INTRUDER/REVISED

Knocking Cancer Out!

By

Reschelle Means

Dedication

To Frank, one of the greatest warriors that I know; the visit that I had with you awakened something in me that I truly can't explain. Your poise and your grace to handle adversities encouraged me so much and showed me what it truly means to appreciate this gift of life. Somehow you managed to encourage me, when I really thought I was there to encourage you. Your presence alone brought peace to my troubled heart, and I will never forget what I learned from you that day. God bless you and your family Frank Hilliard!

Acknowledgment

First and foremost, I would like to thank God for being my strength and my guide in writing this book. I realized how true this gift of writing is for me. You have given me the power to believe in my passion and pursue my dreams. I could never have done this without the faith that I have in You. I love You, my Savior my Friend!

To my wonderful husband, who is incredibly smart and a great visionary, in the words of the great John Legend, (All of me, Loves all of You) sums up my feeling for you. Your love, encouragement and coaching was a tremendous help to me during the process of writing this book.

To my family; My mother; Hattie Shippy, My brothers; Xavier, Jonathan, Jeffrey and Quayne, My sisters; Kalisha, Angela and Tabitha. You are the people who bring me happiness each and every day. Thank you for your listening ear and constant encouragement. I'm so grateful and overjoyed by the love of you all.

To the Big Brother Big Sister Program of the Upstate and Coquita Glass for the opportunity to be a big sister to Jamila Brandon for over 14 years. God knew the bond that would be created between us would last beyond this lifetime. We have laughed, cried, shared stories and learned so much from each other. Your presence in my life is truly an unexplainable gift from God.

To my team of brilliant and smart friends/editors, Sheika Rouse, Jamie Hogue, Serenthia Ross Gartrell, Angela Geter, Regina Hamiliton, Samantha Overton, and Sharonda Brewer thank you ladies, you all are my insightful editors. I am extremely grateful for your patience, your kindness, your brilliance, and always saying yes anytime I needed more assistance. This book would not be possible without you all. My deepest appreciation and gratitude goes to some very special friends; Roxanne Bradley, Tawana Hackett and Bonita Irby. You ladies are a true inspiration to me, your prayers, kindness, encouragement and laughter means everything to me. I am truly blessed to have such a special bond with each of you, I love you all.

I would like to thank Ron Goode, Edward Williams CEO/Owner of KINGDOMATIK VISIONZ and CEE Greenville Boxing Fitness Club and Academic Success Center for the beautiful pictures, and allowing me to use your facility to share in the absolute best photo shoot that I've ever done, I'm ever so grateful!

I wish to express my gratitude to Sharonda Brewer who worked so hard and diligently on designing my book covers. Your great attitude and gracious words *of "yes mam"* anytime I asked you to do something, are forever embedded in my heart. I love and appreciate you more than I can say!

To my wonderful in-laws, thank you all so much for the Sunday and holiday dinners, the Christmas vacations as well as the love and laughter that we share every time were together. I'm so grateful to be a part of your lives. I love you all!

Your body's ability to heal is greater than anyone has ever permitted you to believe.

OH LORD MY GOD, I CRIED OUT TO YOU AND YOU HEALED ME

Psalms 30:2

Table of Contents

Introduction

Have you ever wondered why the body of Christ suffers from so much sickness and disease? You hear every Sunday the list of those that are sick being read off the sick and the shut in. The Pastor, deacons and church members visit and offer prayers, but the fact of the matter remains, sickness is still a huge part of the church. This is a situation that has frustrated me for years. Could it be that our faith is not strong enough to believe that we can actually lay hands on the sick and they will recover? Could it be that we are caught up in the world's system of doing things. The world says, if you are sick go to a physician to take the prescribed medication and it will make you all better. Have you ever thought to consider the side effects of what you are being asked to take? Have you done your research on the medication? In this book you will learn about the dangers of trusting in man and not in God. I'm not saying not to trust your physician, but our ultimate faith should be in God.

I believe when we turn to anything other than God first we run the risk of going down avenues and dealing with situations that weren't necessarily intended for us to go through. Whatever situation you find yourself in trust God, wait and allow Him to lead you. In this book, you will learn of my up and down struggles of dealing with cancer and refusing the standard treatments. Please pay special attention to the words that I used and who I chose to listen to, as I relied solely on the word of God, all the while putting my faith into action to bring about my healing. You will learn how I knocked cancer out!

Chapter One

A Stressful Time

It is not intended for us to know the future. However, God is calling us to walk in faith. It's during this time that we began to grow spiritually causing this outer shell, which means our flesh will begin to crack, crumble and eventually fall away as the new person within starts to develop and emerge. As I considered the sufferings of Jesus, I gained insight into my own pain. My character as well as my faith was on trial, and the only way that I could make it through was by completely surrendering to God and the process at hand.

It was the first week in the month of December 2009. I had to complete two more exams and I would be done with school until the New Year. I was truly in the holiday spirit; bursting with excitement to decorate my home and do some Christmas shopping. I remember driving in my car listening to the beautiful Christmas songs that made the Holiday season that much sweeter. Things begin to turn around quickly. One afternoon while I was out shopping, I received a call from my sister telling me she was taking our mother to the ER. Apparently my mother had been experiencing severe pains in her side that none of my family was aware of.

I remember dropping everything and rushing to the hospital. By the time I arrived, the doctors were running a series of tests to identify the problem. This was a disturbing time for my family, as we had never known our mom to be in the hospital aside from the delivery of her children. After waiting several hours, the doctors informed us that our mother had a bad gallbladder.

Not only was her gallbladder bad, but it was surrounded by what the doctor described as a *"swarm of veins"*. Because of the swarm of veins, removing my mother's gallbladder was a huge risk; one cut vein could cause her to bleed to death.

This news caused my family, as well as myself to be completely frantic. We didn't know what to think. All we could do was pray and ask God to let her be alright. Because the hospital had never seen a medical situation like my mother's, she was transferred to Greenville Memorial Hospital where she was admitted and more tests were underway. My mother's condition had the doctor's baffled. It was as if the doctors were spinning their wheels trying to figure out how to approach the situation.

My family and I continued to pray as we believed God would work it out. After spending days at the hospital, my body began to show signs of stress. While my family remained at the hospital, I returned to school to complete my final two exams, which by the strength of God I passed.

It seemed as if the hours and days were growing longer as we waited to see how the doctors were going to handle my mother's condition. The waiting really tried my patience as we waited anxiously for any sign of hope that they would be able to remove the gallbladder successfully.

Nothing seemed to change. The doctors still didn't know what to think, and as time went on we grew more concerned. We leaned on each other and the healing power of God to get us through. My mother stayed in the hospital for four days before the doctors decided to forgo surgery and release her. By this time Christmas was only a few weeks away. That year I decided to truly splurge; picking up gifts for just about everyone I knew. I don't know what I was thinking, but despite all that was going on; I still had the Christmas spirit.

Even though my mother was out of the hospital, my stress level was still at an all-time high, and my sleep level at an all-time low. In spite of it all, I felt compelled to keep going. I had so much to get done and so little time to do it in. My mind and body were running on fumes. I can recall being in places and wondering how I'd gotten there.

My social calendar was overflowing with my husband and I attending dinner party after dinner party. In fact, the week before Christmas, my husband and I had something planned every day of the week except that Saturday. I had planned to take that day to rest, as I had been experiencing some aches and pains in my body. In fact unbeknownst to my husband, I'd been experiencing chest pains for the past three days. When the chest pains became completely unbearable, I decided to tell my husband and he immediately took me to the ER.

Because of my complaints of chest pain, I was taken back to be seen fairly quickly. While in the ER the doctor took blood, did x-rays, and ordered an EKG; everything came back normal. He asked me what was going on in my life. After I told him, he suggested that I was under a great amount of stress and indicated that stress can cause pain in the chest wall, and I should take it easy for a while and take Ibuprofen. With getting very little rest the previous evening and after leaving the ER, my husband and I left for Florida the next morning, where we stayed for four days fellowshipping with his family. Being a new wife, I hadn't had the opportunity to get to know my husband's family on a personal level and this trip gave me the opportunity to do that through leisurely activities such as, cooking and playing games. It was a wonderful time, but I still found no time to rest. My body was extremely stressed and exhausted. I tried to ignore the weariness I felt, because I had every intention on enjoying the time away with my new family. I had a great Christmas and created beautiful memories with my new in-laws.

By the time the New Year approached, I was looking forward to some rest and all the fullness that the New Year would bring. On January 9th we celebrated my husband's 39th birthday with dinner and friends. A couple of days later, my mother was admitted back into the hospital as a result of the same pain in her side. We knew it had to be her gallbladder since the doctors didn't correct the issue the first time. My mother was again referred back to Greenville Memorial Hospital, and I began to re-live her first experience all over again. We stayed with her until around 10:00 PM that night.

My mother was very exhausted and so was I. She insisted that we all go home in spite of our hesitation to leave her, so that everyone could get some rest. It seemed like the night hours passed by very quickly and when we arrived at the hospital the next day, a whole new protocol was in place. We were shocked to learn that the doctors were planning to do surgery momentarily. I know that news frightened her, as it did us also. I had never been so afraid in my life. My mother has always been the back bone of my immediate family, and I couldn't image what I would do without her. Finally the doctors came and took her to the back, and prepped her for surgery. As we waited for the surgery to be over with, fear and anxiety took over. We had to believe that all the prayers we sent up, God was going to protect her and bring her through.

At last, the surgery was over and it was a complete success. We glorified God because we knew it was because of Him. We were able to breathe easier and get back to our normal day to day happenings. My siblings and I took turns staying with our mother during her recovery and within weeks, she was back on her feet.

Chapter Two

My Discovery

On January 15th my husband and I headed to Winston Salem, NC to attend a Fast Start School. This is a school that we would attend every quarter and its purpose is to teach you how to build a successful business. That's where my journey really began. I thought for sure that everything was smooth sailing since my mother had her surgery and was doing well. As long as she was ok, I felt I could handle anything else that came my way. But little did I know, I was about to walk into what would seem like a nightmare that I couldn't awake from.

The drive to Winston Salem with my husband was pleasant and peaceful. We arrived at the hotel that evening around 6:00 PM. We had just enough time to get our bags up to the room and get unpacked before my husband needed to head down stairs to his meeting with the other Regional Vice Presidents from the surrounding areas.

I stayed in the room and relaxed while he went to his meeting. I was in a different environment and had no plans except to unwind and relax. That evening I remember lying around watching television, talking with my family and friends on the phone, and doing some work on my computer. It was a perfect evening. As the hour was getting late, I went to take a shower. As I was washing, I felt some tenderness in my right thigh. I remember thinking to myself, *"what in the world is this?"* As I touched the area, I felt a small knot.

I continued to shower, but the thought of the knot I'd found lingered in my mind. When my husband returned I told him of my discovery. He could see I was very concerned and told me we would have it checked out by the doctor when we returned home. Even though he said we would have it checked, I still don't believe he took me seriously. He told me later that he thought the knot probably came from my being clumsy around the house. He thought that perhaps I had run into a dresser or something; which I usually did from time to time. I continued to monitor the knot as the days went by, but it never went away.

We continued our weekend in Winston Salem and had a wonderful time. When I returned home I went to the doctor about a week later. I praise God for being all knowing because I had just gotten health insurance on January 4th. I'd received an unexpected phone call from an insurance company about purchasing insurance. I knew I needed it, but hadn't gotten around to getting any. I had no idea at the time of purchase that it would be much needed, but God knew and He had gone before me making provision.

The Initial Process

I initially went to my family doctor, who after poking his finger into my thigh and pressing down on the knot, thought it was a small cyst, but couldn't be sure. He then made an appointment for me to have x-rays done. As I was having the x-rays done, I thought it was a bit strange that the technician was standing behind a glass wall. Little did I know he was protecting himself from the radiation. I had to lie flat on my back, as the beams of radiation flowed through my body.

I didn't quite understand what was going on, but I knew it wasn't good. The results of my x-rays showed *"a bunch of tissues"* as the nurse described it.

In all of this I remember thinking, *"Wow, this sounds kind of serious."* In the next couple of days, my husband and I would return to a different doctor for the third time. The next doctor was a very nice surgeon, who seemed to have more insight to my problem. I tried my best to stay focused and told myself not to worry, because I knew God was with me. The doctor had me undress as he pressed his finger into the knot. By this time, the knot had grown larger and more tender. The doctor suggested that the knot was a lymph node and would possibly go away with an antibiotic.

The doctor prescribed me a ten-day course of antibiotics in the hopes that the treatment would dissolve the lymph node. However, if the antibiotic treatment did not work, he told me the next step would be surgery, followed by a biopsy. By this time I'm thinking, *"What? Surgery and a biopsy, are you serious?"* When I heard him say the word *"biopsy"* I almost fell out of my chair. Anytime I've heard of someone having a biopsy, it was always a serious matter. I hated needles, and all I could think about was the anesthesia.

At that point, I had all kinds of thoughts racing through my mind. Maybe I had been watching too much television, but for some strange reason I was worried that when I was under the anesthesia the doctors would try and take advantage of me. I know, silly thinking right? I told you I had all kinds of thoughts going through my mind.

Nevertheless, my mind had gotten the best of me. I hadn't even tried the prescription to see if it was going to remove the node. I had to encourage myself and pull it together. I eventually got the prescription filled and took it for 10 days as directed. I was certain it would do what it was prescribed to do, which was dissolve the lymph node. I prayed and asked God to cover me. Sure enough, after the 10 days was up the lymph node had gotten smaller, but was still present.

Since the lymph node was still there, I knew the next step was surgery. It took me awhile to digest having to go under the knife. I'd never had surgery before, and frankly I was terrified at the thought of it. On March 4th I had surgery, followed by a biopsy. I felt the peace and assurance of God that all was going to be well. I reminded myself of the scripture, *"He that dwelleth in the secret place of the Most High shall abide under the shadow of the Almighty"* (Psalms 91:1). God's Word gave me comfort.

My husband was right by my side supporting me as I was called back and placed into the prepping room. The nurse in charge walked in and began to prepare me mentally for the process and everything else that would take place. I was told the surgery would take about forty-five minutes. After having the surgery and the anesthesia wearing off, I remember feeling very groggy and somewhat afraid. My family and my friend Hattie was there waiting with my husband. I couldn't believe there had been an actual surgical procedure done on me, because I wasn't in any pain. A biopsy was immediately performed on the lymph node removed from my thigh. Little did I know, while I was under the anesthesia the doctors told my family that the lymph node looked very suspicious.

My family kept this from me because they didn't want to upset me, and I could understand why. My faith was being tested, as I waited over a week for the results of the biopsy to come back. As the days passed, the more nervous I became. I kept praying it was nothing serious, but truly I was at the mercy of my God.

The surgery was over before you know it. I had to remove the bandage covering the scar to remind myself that I had surgery. It was unbelievable. I had a huge scar on my thigh; it was evident that I had the surgery, but felt absolutely no pain. The hardest part was over, or so I thought. As I waited, I realized a week had passed.

I called the doctor's office to inquire about why I had not heard anything about my results. Every time I called, a different nurse gave me a different story. At the time of the procedure, I was told it would be around three or four days before the results would be in, and it was now around the fifth or sixth day. I became very anxious, and started to think there must be something seriously wrong since the doctor hadn't called me. Fear gripped me, while at the same time trying hold on to my faith. Finally, the nurse called me one morning around 8:00 AM and asked my husband and I to come in to the doctor's office around noon.

A huge knot formed in the pit of my stomach as I remembered the doctor's words to me, "*Mrs. Means, if the biopsy comes back normal, we will give you a call with the results over the phone; however, if we find an issue, you will need to come back into the office.*" I was very concerned at that point. I started to panic; going over and over in my mind wondering what could the doctor possibly tell me. After all, it was only a small knot and I thought to myself, *"How serious can it be?"* What the doctor were about to tell me, I would have never guessed it in a million years.

Chapter Three

Completely Shocked

As my husband, mother, sister, and I sat there waiting to hear from the doctor. I had no idea what he was going to tell us. I just knew that it wasn't good. My mind was racing and my emotions were everywhere. However, I was really grateful for the love and support of my family. As the door slowly opened, my heart started beating faster and faster. The doctor walked in the room and said very calmly, *"You have Hodgkin's disease which is a type of cancer."* It seemed in that moment everything stopped, including the clock, and quiet filled the room. My family and I were more shocked than anything. None of us expected the diagnoses would be cancer.

I asked the doctor, *"What is Hodgkin's disease?"* I was under the impression it was a disease that targeted the elderly. The doctor informed me that Hodgkin's disease was a type of cancer that attacks the lymphatic system. It can show up in both young and old men and women. I needed to be certain that I'd heard the doctor correctly so I asked, *"Are you saying that I have cancer?"* With a pained look on his face, the doctor replied, *"Yes."* God was in the midst of the situation, He had to be because otherwise, I would have passed out right then and there. I was definitely in a state of shock as I attempted to digest what was being said to me.

My mind went into process mode as my family began to ask several different questions. Dr. Tate, who was the surgeon and an excellent doctor, was very calm as he tried to explain the diagnosis in more detail. My mother immediately said, *"I rebuke that in the name of Jesus!"* My husband stood calmly, listening very careful as the doctor explained the disease further. When the doctor walked out of the room, my sister looked up Hodgkin's disease on her iPhone and told us the disease had a very high survival rate. Although, I later found out that a good friend of mine's father had just died from Hodgkin's disease.

As the doctor walked out, one of the nurses walked in and said to us, *"Out of all the cancer's, Hodgkin's is one of the most curable out there. If a person just had to have cancer, this is the one to have because it's not only treatable but curable."* That was refreshing to hear, but to me, cancer was still cancer and I didn't want to have anything to do with it. My husband and family were a great support, and from that moment on, we prayed and asked God to show us the way. I think my family on one hand felt a great sadness for me, and on the other hand great hope because of the survival rate.

On the way from the surgeon's office, we stopped to schedule an appointment with Gibbs Cancer Center. While outside, my husband immediately called his mother and told her the diagnosis. In that moment he expressed his great sorrow and hurt. I had never seen him break down and cry like that. My heart ached so bad to see him in that much pain. There was complete silence on the drive home. It was as if we were both frozen with shock and without words to speak. The word *"intruder"* kept ringing in my spirit. I could not understand what that meant. Little did I know Intruder would be the title of my first book.

Lord, I Need You

The next day, as things became clearer and the shock wore off, I heard the word *"invasion."* I began to rationalize in my mind that somehow I had left the door open for the enemy to walk right in. As the days turned to weeks, I continued to examine myself. I continuously went over the scenario in my head asking myself, *"What caused this? Was it something I ate or drank? Was it something I did or didn't do?"* Needless to say, I was at a place where only God could help me. I turned to Him and began to confess sins that were in my life. In my mind, I just wanted to be right with God because I needed Him now more than ever. I was in a state of desperation, and perhaps that is what sparked my innate need for confession. As I reflected back over my life, I knew I did the right thing.

God is so holy, and in order to come before Him, you must come clean with Him, confessing any sins. I needed the pathway to be clear; I needed the heavens to open up on my behalf. I was willing to do whatever it took to get into His presence. The ultimate fight for my life had begun. I was so serious that nothing was going to keep me from getting into the presence of God. I began repenting for other people's sin, I was plain and out right desperate. It wasn't that I was living a life immersed in sin, but I'd been so distracted by everything that had previously gone on in my life that I began to neglect my relationship with God. I wasn't praying and studying His word as I had been accustomed to. I didn't want to believe this illness was of God. Nevertheless, He allowed this affliction so it must have been for a good reason. I wasn't mad at God. I just knew it was something that my family and I were going to have to deal with. As days went by I grabbed a hold of God's extended hand, choosing to put all my trust in Him and walk as closely as I could to Him. I heard the diagnosis but refused to accept it. I grew up in a household where illness was not accepted. Perhaps it was because my mother worked in the healthcare field and worked around sick people all day. When she would come home from work, she didn't want to see anymore sickness. Whatever aches or pains we had, absolutely had to be gone by the time she came home. This may seem like a cold and heartless attitude to have, but that's how I was brought up and that's what shaped my mentality concerning sickness. My mother wouldn't accept it and neither would I.

I remember returning home from the doctor's office the day of the diagnosis and the internet was not working, which was strange. I wanted to research Hodgkin's disease and find out more of what it entailed. It took about four days for the internet to come back up, so instead I went to the office and started researching everything I could on Hodgkin's. That was a huge mistake. I truly believe God allowed the internet to be down for a reason. By the time I got off the computer, I was a colossal mess. Some of the things I read online disturbed me, and needless to say I became very fearful. My husband saw me on the computer and knew exactly what I was doing. He suggested that I get off of the computer at that moment. Because of the fear, I needed to think. Honestly, I didn't know what I was going to do.

Chapter Four

God Will Guide You

A few moments later I drove to the park. It was a place I would always go to think and pray. It was my place of refuge and safety. When I arrived, I sat in my car and cried out to God repeatedly, *"No, Lord please this can't be happening!"* I sat there for about forty-five minutes, sobbing uncontrollably then suddenly, my tears dried up. I felt the peace of God like never before. The Holy Spirit prompted me to call a good friend of mine. I called First Lady Reva and began to explain to her the doctor's report. She immediately told me what to do. Her mother had previously been diagnosed with breast cancer and was being treated with natural and herbal supplements.

First Lady Reva suggested that I purchase some Barley Powder, Japanese Mushroom Vitamins, and Aloe Vera Juice from the Whole Food Store. She also told me they prayed over her mom day in and day out. They would anoint her daily and made sure the Word of God was being deposited into her spirit. I felt so much better after speaking with First Lady because she shared with me some thing's I could do. I left the park and went back to my husband's office. When I walked in he noticed right away that my attitude was different. He heard hope in my voice. I told him what First Lady had told me and that I was going to the store to purchase the items she suggested.

When I got to the Whole Food Store, my first question to the store associate was, *"What is good to take if the doctor says someone has cancer?"* The associate referred me to a woman named

Lorena. I asked her the same question. She asked me, *"Who has cancer?"* I told her, *"The doctors say that I have it."* I want to pause right here and speak to you, the reader, directly. Notice I said *"the doctors (they) say" I have cancer."* NEVER claim something you don't want. The cancer wasn't mine, and I was not about to claim it. As I was saying, Lorena suggested Barley Powder, Aloe Vera Juice, Mushroom Vitamins and some other things. Everything she suggested was on the list that First Lady Reva had given to me. I knew right then that I was in the right place, at the right time, buying the right things. Glory to God!

Lorena also shared with me that she was diagnosed with Thyroid Cancer about 10 years earlier and refused chemotherapy, surgery and radiation, and there was no cancer in her system. I thought to myself, *"What?"* I couldn't believe that God had led me to a person who was able to defeat cancer without the standard treatments of chemotherapy and radiation. I felt even more empowered! I had God on my side and now some proof that there were other ways cancer could be cured. Lorena said she started treating herself with natural herbs and supplements as she changed her diet. She introduced me to a website about raw foods, called Hallelujah Acers. I began to search through this website and learned how to prepare meals and the importance of eating the right foods. Lorena and another employee named Mike were extremely helpful in answering my many questions. For every question, they had an answer.

I purchased all the items that were suggested to me. When I left the Whole Food Store, I'd spent about $70 and walked away with one small bag. It was crazy, but that was the best $70 I had ever spent. It was there that I learned if I had been exercising, eating right, and drinking plenty of water, I could have alleviated the lymph node in the first place. I was advised to cut out all sugar as sugar and cancer feed on each other. These were all things I felt the doctors should have told me immediately.

I felt the doctors were only interested in the disease and not my personal well-being. I wanted to know how I could get well, but really wasn't getting the answers from the doctor's that I needed. Along with the supplements, I was advised to go on a raw food diet. My initial thought was I didn't understand how anyone could eat raw foods. You may be wondering the same thing. Raw foods meant drinking pure vegetable juice that has been blended with a juicer. Although I did not start juicing immediately, I did immediately cut out all sugar, sodas, bread, fried foods, and basically all meat except baked chicken. Please do not be fooled, this wasn't by any means easy, but for the sake of my health, I couldn't think twice about it. God was already guiding me into my healing.

With the biggest part of my meals being cut I began to lose weight very quickly. Instead of feeling worse because of the cancer, I actually started feeling better. My skin became clearer. I started to feel healthier and stronger than I'd ever felt. Once I stopped eating sugar I didn't feel as weighed down and bloated. My diet before the diagnosis had been pretty horrible, so I was able to see immediate changes in my body once I corrected it.

I also became obsessed with reading God's Word. As I continued to search the scriptures on healing, the promises of God started to come alive as my body was going through transition. God's word alone gives life and provides empowerment.

Finally, the time had come for my first visit at The Cancer Center. When I arrived, the oncologist had my biopsy report and had me scheduled for bone marrow testing. After listening to the doctors, my husband asked the question, *"What does she need to do differently? Does she need to change her diet or anything to help herself get well?"* The oncologist's exact words were, *"Oh no, she can continue to eat what she has been eating, because with this type of cancer, it doesn't matter what she eats."* I knew right then that I couldn't trust the doctors. I couldn't figure out why he would tell us that. I remembered what I was told at the Whole Food Store. My eating habits should have been the first thing the doctors suggested that I change.

The oncologist gave me no advice as to how I could help myself get well. The more I talked with people, and the more I began to research, I saw that there were all sorts of things I could have done differently, and could still do to get well. At first, I really thought the doctors were trying to kill me, even though at that time the doctors hadn't mentioned chemotherapy or radiation; I knew they were the treatment options used to treat cancer. The treatments the doctors would use would keep me sick and thus expenses would be at an all-time high. I felt they offered treatments, but couldn't guarantee a positive outcome. It didn't take me long to figure out it was all about money.

I had to lay aside all of my previous assumptions about how I ate and took care of myself and start all over. I was at a point where everything I thought was right, was actually wrong. I needed God to give me discipline and to show me how to take care of myself. I also needed His strength and courage for the challenge I was faced with.

As time passed, I gained a little more peace since I now had all the things I needed to get well. I had a world of information at my fingertips, because of the internet and I intended on finding out as much as I could about this disease. My mission and main focus became walking in divine health. My oncologist suggested that I do five weeks of radiation, five days a week. At the time, my husband and I thought, at least it wasn't chemotherapy.

The day had finally arrived for the bone marrow testing. Since the doctors said the cancer was in my lymph nodes, they wanted to be sure it hadn't traveled into my bones and spleen. Now I have to honestly say that test was the most painful experience I had ever had. I've heard people talk about the test and how bad it was, but it was even worse than what I'd imagined. During the test all I could do was lie there as the tears rolled down my face. My husband was very supportive and caring during the test. He stood by my side the entire time, holding my hand and encouraging me to be strong as he watched the oncologist drill a needle the length of a pencil into my back.

The oncologist was a very short man, so he had to stand up over me on a stool in order to dig the marrow out of my back. I was given a very painful shot in the lower left side of my back that was supposed to numb me so I wouldn't feel anything when the marrow was removed; however, I'm certain I felt far more than I was supposed to. The oncologist told me I had strong bones so he had to apply three times the pressure into my lower back, digging deeper and deeper to remove the marrow. All the while a nurse stood by wiping the sweat off of his brow. You would have thought he was a mechanic or something, it just seemed like too much labor and I was the car that he was working on.

Finally, after about 20 minutes the marrow was removed. Praise God! I could see the doctor was exhausted from all the pressure he had to apply. I believe that was more work than he and I both anticipated. But thank God the test was complete.

I wasn't able to walk so my husband had to help me up the stairs. When we opened the door my little sister Jamila was there. I was so happy to see her. She has always been the sunshine in my day. She stayed for an hour or so and had to leave; all I could do for the next day and a half was stay in bed.

The night of the bone marrow test, my husband had a big meeting with a lot of new people joining him in business. He was reluctant about going and leaving me in my condition, but I insisted that he go, as I would be okay. I stayed in bed and slept the rest of the evening. I took advantage of the rest, as I prepared myself mentally for the results of the bone marrow test as well as more tests that I'd have soon.

I was scheduled a couple of weeks out to have PET and CT scans done. The purpose of the scans was to see how far the cancer had spread throughout my body. As I waited for the time to have the scans done, I continued to focus on eating right and making sure I was in the right frame of mind. I was very hopeful that if I did everything I was supposed to do, when the time would come for me to take the test, by faith I believed the cancer would not be present. I was on an all-out prowl, seeking and researching everything I could get my hands on. I was determined that this cancer was getting out of my body!

Faith That Moves

I started sowing seeds into Dr. Mike Murdock's ministry. If you believe God for anything, I encourage you to activate your faith! Look for ways and opportunities to sow seeds, meaning giving of your time, or resources to be a blessing to someone else. The principle of sowing and reaping doesn't fail. If you sow, you will reap. God's Word does not lie. I was faithful concerning taking my supplements along with drinking plenty of water and getting regular exercise. I felt really good about everything I was doing.

After the diagnosis by the doctors, people kept telling me all kinds of stories about their loved ones who had died from cancer. One lady shared with me that she'd lost three friends to breast cancer in one year. Another person told me he had recently lost two cousins. It seemed like death was all around me, all I kept hearing about were fatalities. Where were the survival stories? Everyone knew someone who had died of cancer and all those who I heard about took chemotherapy.

That has always been my first question when someone dies of

cancer, *"did they take chemotherapy or radiation?"* It appeared to me the treatments were associated with death. I don't fault anyone for sharing their experiences with me, but I had to listen and not perceive. I couldn't allow my mind to focus on death. Most people who hear the word cancer immediately equate it to a death sentence. I think every time a person hears about another person's cancer diagnosis, it is inevitable for them to want to share with you who they know that has cancer, as well as everyone who have died from it. However, don't allow their stories to frighten you and cause you to lose your faith.

Listen and be compassionate as we are supposed to, but know that every situation is different. Also, remember that God has already made provision for your healing. The Bible says that He took our infirmities and bore our sickness. Provision has been made for you. Your sins are forgiven, grace has been supplied, your body is healed, you have access to the peace of God, and the list of Gods promises goes on and on. Since by His stripes you are healed, accept His provision as truth, and stand on God's word.

I also had to eliminate distractions. I had to remove from my life people and things that were negative. Just hearing the doctor say I had cancer was dreadful enough; I absolutely didn't need people or things around me that would bring my spirit down. Believe it or not, the television can be just a detrimental as having negative people in your life. It can be difficult to remain positive and hopeful when a vast amount of shows on the television promote so much violence and negative images. These types of shows cause a disturbance in your spirit.

"And we know that we are of God and the whole world lies under the sway of the wicked one (1John 5:19). Under the power of Satan, eyes have been blinded and many don't believe he exists. The enemy uses deception to rule the world; Jesus said the devil does not stand in the truth. I know it may sound crazy to some, but when I was told I had cancer, I felt it was a lie and it was of the devil. I truly believed that sickness was not of God.

You may be wondering, who is in control of the world, is it God or Satan? Jesus said, *"All Power is given unto Me in heaven and in earth"* (Matthew 28:18). For a short period of time, Satan has full range to seek, devour, and cause as much disturbance and chaos as he can until his appointed time of destruction in the lake of fire.

The enemy is doing his best to cause the people of God to fall and doubt God, but you must hold on and keep your faith strong. Most people give up just when they are on the verge of a breakthrough. I heard a prominent Pastor once say, *"Most people weather the wind and the waves of the storm only to die at the shore."* You never know how close you are, so get a grip on your mind and keep standing in faith.

What you see and constantly hear has a major effect on where you are in your life, especially in your mind. To this day, I don't watch television much at all. When my husband comes home from the office I may watch a bit of television then for the sake of spending time with him. Other than that, I have learned to turn it off, or watch something that is inspirational and uplifting. I'm not trying to come off as overly holy or deep, but the fact is, we have control over what we allow in our spirits. Between the spirit and the flesh, whichever one you feed the most, is the one that grows the most. It's important to keep your spirit fed.

Chapter Five

Our Desires

I read an online article by a guy named Wayne who wrote about how advertising creates the desire to want more in a society that doesn't understand the meaning of need. After reading that article I began to take notice of the many commercials and billboards that advertise foods saturated with fat and sugar. Fast foods are loaded with all sorts of harmful preservatives that are dangerous to our bodies; it's no wonder chronic diseases such as; hypertension, diabetes, and cancer are on the rise. Commercials and advertising only make the problem worse. We are living in a society without discipline.

To put it quite candidly, it's not just the commercials, it's the people who have no knowledge of the tricks of the enemy, so when bad things are being promoted, we think it's good. It's things that look good to us but are actually bad for us that cause so much disease and death. The desire to want more and more comes from people who have no need, but because they see it, they have to have it whether it's good for them or not. I truly believe that we as a society sometimes don't realize the harm we inflict upon ourselves. I know I certainly didn't. Until I was diagnosed I ate whatever I wanted, whenever I wanted it.

I drank plenty of sodas, didn't eat many fruits or vegetables, did absolutely no exercise and I drank very little water. These are all the things the body needs to defend itself against disease. Please hear me, if you are a person who puts no thought into what you and your family is eating, you could be causing great harm to yourself and your loved ones. I didn't write this to scare you, but to be honest and perhaps give you an *"aha"* moment. I wish dearly that someone had told me what I'm telling you. Healthy eating is very important whether your goal is to lose weight or to just provide your body with the proper fuel it needs to be run smoothly.

This battle with cancer has made me more compassionate and more aware of the pain in the world. It allowed me to understand fear and heartache in an incomprehensible fashion. Even though I experienced the emotion that sometimes caused me to fear, I had complete assurance that God was able to do more than my mind could conceive. *"Now unto him that is able to do exceeding abundantly above all that we ask or think, according to the power that worketh in us"*(Ephesians 3:20). The first question you must ask yourself is; *do you believe that God is able?* His word declares that He is. In the above scripture we are informed that God is able to do exceeding and abundantly above! You may be asking, *"Exceeding and abundantly above what?"* Anything we can ask or are able to think of. God can perform acts that we could never comprehend regardless of how hard we tried. He is God! His ways and thoughts are higher than ours.

Caught Off Guard

"But through it all and the peace of God which surpasses all understandings will guard your hearts and your mind in Christ Jesus" (Philippians 4:7). I remember one particular incident where I was resting in the peace of God and the enemy was attempting to attack my mind, making me think that something was wrong with

me for not worrying. I was at home with no worries or fear at that time, and sure enough the enemy began placing thoughts into my mind like: *"You know you should be worrying because cancer is a deadly disease that many people die from!"*

Instead of casting down those thoughts and feelings, I made a call to my friend Roxanne to ask her if it was normal for me not to worry about the report the doctors gave. I told her that I felt like I should be worried, but I wasn't and her exact words to me were: *"You tell that devil that you don't even understand the peace that you have so you know he doesn't, and that he better back up off you!"* By that time I was pumped up! I said, *"Yea, that's right devil, I don't even understand this peace that I have, so I know you don't. You better back up off me!"*

I got so tickled at her words, but they were so true and sure enough, those words put the devil under my feet. When the devil tries to prey on you and make you think you should be in a state of worriment when you know you have peace, quickly cast him down. Don't do like I did at that time, listen to him and then question if having peace is possible. The Word of God tells us *"He will keep us in perfect peace whose mind is stayed on Thee"* (Isaiah 26:3).

This was a tactic of the enemy to keep me fearful, but thank God in that moment, I had a friend close by to encourage me. I was told on numerous occasions that loved ones had found spots on the lungs, cancer on the brain, and every other place that cancer could dwell. God was on the scene, but so was the enemy. I was doing everything that I could to stay encouraged. I was literally fighting the good fight of faith. Some moments I found myself to be very strong, but then there were times I felt defeated.

How Long?

You may be in a situation right now that you're asking God, how long? David would often ask God, *"How long will You hide your face from me? How long will the enemy triumph over me?* One minute David is praising God for showing Himself mighty and the next minute David is grieved and wondering when God is going to show up. David was a man after God's own heart, although he had fears, God loved him so much. This is the same love He has for you and me. He will never let us down.

If God allowed you to go through something, I guarantee He has already equipped you. You are stronger than you think you are. He knows us. He knows when our faith is being shaken and when we are about to fold. Yet He continues to walk and guide us through. I love the poem, *The Footprints in the Sand;* because it's during those tough times we look back and see how God has been carrying you and I.

It's not only about cancer; it could be any disease or any hardship that you may be going through. God's got you in the palm of His hand. Be encouraged, because the devil will cause you to fear at times just as he did David. But just know the devil does not operate in the truth.

Chapter Six

A Word of Confirmation

I received a phone call early one Saturday morning from my Aunt Sheila who asked me to read Ezekiel 47:12. I immediately opened my Bible, and the Scripture read, *"Along the bank of the river, on this side and that, will grow all kinds of trees used for food; their leaves will not wither, and their fruit will not fail. They will bear fruit every month because their water flows from the sanctuary. Their fruit will be for food and their leaves for medicine."*

That scripture excited me so much and gave me zeal to keep moving forward. I'd never read that particular scripture before and was so grateful that she called and asked me to read it. The Scripture was in alignment with what I was already doing, which was eating the foods of the earth and allowing it to heal me. It felt good to know that I was on the right track. After all, the oncologist hadn't even mentioned chemotherapy, yet I was being very proactive. I couldn't leave any stone unturned. It became my focus to knock cancer out!

My faith was elevated all the more, because I now had a scripture to back up what I was doing. I had been defiling my temple for years. So many times we think defilement only comes from acts such as sex outside of marriage or drinking, but putting the wrong foods in our body is a form of defilement as well. We wonder why there's so much sickness on the earth. Before we start to blame doctors or others, we need to examine ourselves; people die from ignorance every day. Learning and applying is the key.

The next day my family and friends gathered for prayer. My aunt anointed and laid hands on me. My brother led us in prayer. The presence of God filled the room, and His spirit assured me that all was well. I kept reminding myself of the Scripture, "For *I know the thoughts that I have for you, says the Lord, plans to prosper you, to give you a future and a hope"* (Jeremiah 29:11). I had to believe God was not going to allow this sickness to be the end of me, and that His ultimate master plan for my life would come forth to bring about His glory.

Words that Really Hurt

As the weeks turned into a month, I spoke to one of my family members on the phone, his first question was, *"You're not dead yet?"* It was as if my heart dropped and I experienced a pain that I had never felt before. Hearing those words was worse than hearing the diagnosis. My family has the tendency to joke a lot, so I know the comment was not made to be taken seriously, but the words hurt nonetheless. We must be careful not to add to a person's pain. If you've never experienced something and can't sympathize just say, *"Continue to trust God, or hold on to His promise."* We must be ready at all times for God to use us, even if it's giving a word of encouragement. I was given an apology for the un-kind words that were spoken to me, and of course I accepted the apology, but the words still left its stain. I was the only person in the family who had ever been diagnosed with cancer. After all, I grew up in a family where there was no compassion for sickness.

All I could do to keep my mind together was pray and trust God.

I found God to be a refuge in the time of trouble. These are not just words, but when things got the most challenging for me, I chose to meditate on His Word and there I found a place of safety. This place of safety is one that you have to get to on your own. Think on His goodness and allow the presence and peace of God to fill your heart and your mind.

More Testing

The time had finally arrived for me to have the scans done. Before the scans were performed, I had to sit in a room and drink a white liquid every thirty minutes. Since the liquid was white, it reminded me of milk, which I hate and it tasted like chalk. The purpose of the liquid was to get a clear look at my colon to be able to determine if there was any cancer in that area. The nurse also injected me with sugar water. This would allow the doctors to see where the cancer was in my body specifically. Remember, sugar causes cancer to spread, which is why it's important to refrain from consuming it.

After about an hour, I transitioned to the next room to have the scans done. The machine that I had to lie in to have the scans done was very large and somewhat intimidating. I was very nervous however; the process turned out to be painless and lasted less than an hour. Now all I had to do was wait for the results as I allowed the patience of God to be developed in me.

While leaving the doctor's office, I met the most beautiful woman with the sweetest spirit I had ever encountered. This woman was full of joy and hope. She started telling me about Noah's ark and how God had dealt with her about being in the ark. She said the ark represented safety. She said God assured her that she was in His care and He was going to bring her through. When she spoke, I listened. She had been through a lot with battling breast cancer for two years. Despite her condition she didn't look, or act sick. I knew she was a classy lady by the way she carried herself. Even with no hair due to the chemo, she elegantly wore a matching hat and scarf set. I could tell that the Lord was with her.

It did my heart good to see her so encouraged and her spirit so uplifted. She had a winner's mindset, and it showed in her attitude. Your mindset is going to be your greatest tool to overcome and defeat anything in this life. *"As a man thinks in his heart so is he"* (Proverbs 23:7). Yes, it is true cancer kills hundreds of thousands of people each year, but there is hope regardless of what type of cancer or what stage the cancer may be in. Knowledge is power. The more knowledgeable I became about this disease, the more I knew I could overcome it. Jesus said, *"He has come that we may have life and have it more abundantly" (John.* 10:10). We are not supposed to be defeated in any area of our lives. Sickness, poverty, failure or struggles, it doesn't matter what the situation is; we are supposed to experience an abundant life, even in our trials.

We can allow our trials to build our character as we grow closer to God. He is always in the business of developing us. He is just as interested in the journey as He is with our destination. As the transformation takes place, it doesn't feel good but it's working for your good. So whatever you are dealing with, be encouraged. God is doing a greater work in you.

Chapter Seven

Focus on Your Future

When I was confused about my journey, God began revealing bits
and pieces of my future. I was totally caught off guard when I was
told I had cancer, but it was a part of the flight. You too may be in a
storm and the flight may not be as smooth. You may feel like you
are going through loops and circles wondering what's going on.
However it's okay, whatever any of us may deal with; God doesn't
waste any of our experiences. We have to stay focused on what God
is doing in us through our times of trials. God is in control and will
perfect that which concerns us.

As I chose to focus on my future, I had to add hope. God sees
your life completed and finished *"Your eyes saw my substance,
being yet unformed, and in Your book they all were written, the days
fashioned for me, when as yet there were none of them"* (Psalms
139:16). God see's your value and is ready to guide you through.

As I waited for the results to come in over the next weeks, I
continued to pray and thank God for my healing. I started doing
confessions and declaring, *"I will live and not die, and declare the
works of the Lord"* (Psalms 118:17). I had to keep my thoughts
positive and was told to keep my future before me. I was determined
that my husband and I would do all the things we had planned to do.
While I waited anxiously for the results of my scans I constantly
reminded myself of God's Word during any moments of fear and
doubt.

Lies and Delusions of the Enemy

The wait time seemed like forever as the devil was busy creating delusions in my mind and body. I would lie in bed at night and have pains moving throughout my body. The pains would literally be in my elbows, back, and knees. The enemy tried to make me think the cancer was spreading. I have a friend named Frank who was diagnosed with cancer also. Wouldn't you know it, he felt pain which was the reason he went to the doctor to get checked in the first place. However, after he was diagnosed with cancer the pain seemed to intensify. I would ask him how he was feeling and he would always say, *"Not good"*. I told him after I was diagnosed I really began to hurt as well, but the pains weren't real. They were only delusions of the enemy to make us think the cancer had spread all over our bodies.

I told myself I wasn't going to focus on the pain, and I suggested to Frank that he shouldn't either. My focal point was Jesus, and the suffering that He faced on the cross and in the garden of Gethsemane. If He suffered for my sins and the sins of the world, than surely I could endure also. I ultimately knew and understood that just like Jesus, there was a greater purpose behind the pain. I believe that our lives should be so submissive to the will of God that we would be unable to say anything but, *"Thy will be done* (Matthew 6:10).

For the first time in the Bible I saw Jesus at His lowest point. He exemplified strength and power everywhere He went, but in the Garden of Gethsemane we read about His agony and His plea for

God to let this cup pass from Him, or in other words remove Him from His situation.

That gave me comfort to know that it was okay for me to feel agony and dread as long as my faith was stronger than my feelings. I knew that I would get through it.

When I returned to the Oncologist to get the results of the scans, I was terrified. It was one thing to know the doctor's say I have cancer, It was another thing to know if the cancer had spread or not. I learned that the cancer was still there even though I prayed that God would remove it. I wasn't really upset; I just knew that I had to keep my faith strong, and continue to move forward. Giving up wasn't an option. I learned the cancer was not only there, but the scans showed another spot on my left thigh. However, the oncologist saw no need to be concerned about the other spot. Praise God we caught it early and the cancer was in stage one, even with the other spot showing up. I was so relieved and thank God the cancer hadn't spread all over my body.

Better to Trust in God

The oncologists scheduled another appointment for me at The Cancer Center in Greenville. There we met Dr. Matthews. She told us that she was concerned about the spot on my other leg. She also informed me that a spot can't just jump from one leg to another leg, but that it had to travel. She stated that the cancer traveled through my lymph system, up my stomach, and back down into my leg, and was no longer stage one as earlier diagnosed, but stage two. She suggested chemotherapy as well as radiation which were completely different from what the previous oncologist suggested. We were definitely at a cross road and completely unsure of which direction to take. My mind was spinning out of control. I was so confused, and the thought of taking chemotherapy really concerned me, and made me question the doctor's concern for my wellbeing.

I told God I was putting all my faith and trust in Him and that I didn't want Him to allow anything to happen to me that He didn't ordain. I put my life in the Lord's hands, because I knew He was my healer. I would respect the doctors for their position, but I chose to trust in God. As time went on, I started to do more research on chemotherapy. My mother and my husband had great concerns and weren't in agreement with me taking the prescribed treatments by the oncologist. I had previously ordered a DVD by Dr. Lorraine Day, titled *"Cancer, You Don't Scare Me."* In the DVD she began to expose the hidden side effects of chemotherapy and radiation.

Her DVD gave me much more insight into the damage these treatments cause to the body. She listed many side effects that the oncologist never mentioned. The oncologist told us that chemo would make all of my hair come out in addition to causing severe nausea and making me very weak. My husband started asking questions like, *"What about chemo destroying the good organs such as, the heart, liver, and lungs?"* The doctors couldn't deny that the treatments could potentially destroy those organs with the possibility of them not rebuilding themselves, and they also couldn't give us any guarantee that the cancer wouldn't come back.

I thought to myself, *"If there is no guarantee, then why would I take that chance and put my life at risk?*" We learned that chemo causes congestive heart failure, severe kidney damage, sores in the mouth, shortness of breath, pneumonia, memory loss, and many other serious side effects that the doctors failed to mention. I pray if you or someone you know is faced with the choice to take chemotherapy that you would do your research before committing to the treatments. Please don't think that the oncologist has your best interest at heart. Some do, but most don't. It's his or her job to offer the standard treatments of radiation, chemotherapy, and surgery. I truly believe that oncologists know that chemotherapy is extremely toxic for the body. I'm sure they see first-hand how much sickness and death it causes from the treatments that are designed to help.

It's not that I don't believe oncologists aren't sincere in their work, I do, I assume they have to suggest what they've been taught. They aren't even allowed to discuss natural medicines. I spoke with several doctors concerning natural and alternative treatments and was given *"no comment"*.

God Intervened

I had been given several diagnoses, and the oncologist wanted to schedule surgery right away to have the port placed in my chest to start chemotherapy. On Friday morning I was scheduled to be back at the oncologist. The doctor's wanted to explain to me the details of the port. However, there was a truck explosion on interstate 85. My husband was coming from our home to meet me at my appointment by 10:00 a.m. I was already in Spartanburg working 3rd shift and

46

would be leaving from work to go to my appointment.

Since my husband was stuck in traffic, I went on to the appointment without him. This would be the first time my husband missed any of my appointments. Praise God for my mother who was able to go in his place. She came by my job early that morning and expressed to me that she wasn't feeling comfortable with me taking the chemotherapy treatments. She was concerned about the serious side effects and advised me not to go that route.

By this time it had been several weeks later and I was emotionally tired. Although I shared the same concerns as her and my husband regarding the treatments, if she had not been there I may have considered getting the port and prepared for the treatments. For a brief moment I got weary, and it seemed easier to give in than to fight. It's in times like those that you will need someone who is able to stand up and fight for you. God used my mother that day to fight for me when it seemed like all of my strength was gone.

When we arrived, the oncologist expressed his concerns about the treatments. I was strongly urged to take chemotherapy along with radiation, and was told I shouldn't gamble with my life. The oncologist then began to make arrangements for me to have surgery and have a port placed in my chest to begin the treatments. My mother immediately said, *"Hold up, I think we need another opinion before we decide to do anything concerning placing ports in her."* Somehow we found out the oncologist I had been seeing specialized in breast cancer. I didn't understand why I was referred to that particular oncologist when I'd been diagnosed with Lymphoma. In our quest for a second opinion concerning the stage two diagnoses, we began asking questions and looking for universities who specialized in the type of cancer I was diagnosed with. We were told about Emory University in Atlanta Georgia and decided to go there for further answers. We found out that Emory had a staff of oncologist's who specialized in Hodgkin's disease. We immediately called the hospital to schedule an appointment. As I spoke with the receptionist, she asked me a series of questions, and then told me she would call back with an appointment date and time.

Took My Eyes off God

In the meantime, as I waited for Emory to call back, I decided I needed to bury myself in God's word. I thought to myself, am *I really going to be able to live day to day knowing this disease is in my body and trust God, and act as if it's not?* It's easy to talk about how much we love and trust God, but when our backs are against the wall, God is watching to see how our faith holds up. Never in a million years would I have guessed that my life would have gone in this direction. God has given to each of us a measure of faith, but this was going to take mega faith. I had to live everyday as if I was already healed until God made it manifest. After all, I had turned down all forms of treatment offered by my oncologist.

My faith was on trial and I had a lot of people watching me. I spent a lot of time in daily prayer. The word of the Lord gave me strength and comfort that I could not have found in any person. For the most part, I had a very positive outlook on the entire situation. I never looked at myself as being sick. The Scripture is proven *"The spirit of a man will sustain him in sickness"* (Proverbs 18:14). God sustained me so much that I never looked sick, I never physically got sick, and even when I had the surgery to remove the lymph node, I never experienced any pain. My greatest challenge was in my mind and dealing with the delusions the enemy created.

Chapter Eight

Your Health Starts From Within

I genuinely believe that all disease originates from within and therefore can only be healed from within. Some may disagree with this statement, but I believe all disease that manifests in the outer, physical body has arisen from within our conscious or subconscious mind. I believe diseases are sometimes the effects of your thoughts and feelings. Stress is also one of the main causes of *"dis-ease"* which results in a lack of ease in the mind and body. If you are constantly stressed, it can manifest in your physical body. If you worry about your health, you will remain unhealthy and your health will eventually deteriorate. You have to understand that being healthy is your natural state of being. It's what we allow that causes our health to worsen. Remember the stress I described earlier in the book, within the next month I noticed the knot in my thigh, and a few months later I was told it was cancer. Every situation is not the same and it's definitely no reason to be afraid. My suggestion is to keep your stress level as low as possible. Stress and worry affects you in ways that you don't even realize.

One quick point before I go on: When you take medicine with the mindset of *"I have a disease and therefore I am taking this medicine for it,"* the medicine reinforces the disease. When you take a medicine while thinking about the disease you are hoping to cure, you are attracting more of the same. But if you believe that taking the medicine will cure you, it will. It's not the substance that's contained in the medicine that brings about the cure, but the belief that it will cure you.

In Total Awe

One day I decided to attend a support group sponsored by The American Cancer Society. It was nice to be around other people who had an understanding for what I was going through. The leader of the group expressed to me how glad she was to have me there. I was offered refreshments while we waited for the rest of the people to get there. To my surprise, the refreshments consist of chocolate chip cookies, brownies and soda.

I thought to myself, *"Why in the world would they serve these types of junk foods to people with this type of illness? These people are trying to kill me and everyone else in this room"* That was my honest thought at the time. Since it was a well-known organization like the American Cancer Society, I felt they of all people should have known better than to serve that type of food. Carrots, celery sticks, or even fruit would have been great options and much healthier than what they were serving. Everyone at the support group had taken chemo and was in remission, yet none of them had any idea as to what harm they were causing themselves by eating such unhealthy foods. God's word is so true *"My people are destroyed for a* lack *of knowledge"* (Hosea 4:6).

They asked me if I had I taken chemo or radiation. I told them I had surgery to remove the lymph node in March and had not taken any treatments. Ms. Laura the facilitator of the group looked at me and said, *"It seems like you have a long way to go."* I remember looking at her and saying, *"I really don't believe that chemo is the route God wants me to take and when God is present, it doesn't have to take long.*" I told them how I had changed my diet and began to look into alternative medicine. Everything I was saying was foreign to them. No one had ever talked to them about anything other than chemo and radiation.

My heart was heavy listening to their stories because so much suffering and pain had already taken place. I think about so many people who have lost their lives and didn't have to because doctors told them, like they told me, "*I strongly urge you to take chemo.*" In the beginning, I genuinely thought chemo was my only option. So many people to this day still think that. I began to ask people if they knew of anyone who had taken chemo. Everyone knew someone who had taken chemo treatments and were either suffering from some other type of illness as a result of the chemo, or who took the treatments and still died. I know there are some people who have taken the chemo treatments and are doing well, like my husband's cousin, Lisa Mitchell. Although, it was still rough for her, God saw her through. She is a part of the 3% survival rate.

You may have different reasons for reading this book. Either you have been diagnosed with cancer, you know someone who is diagnosed with cancer, or you're simply interested in learning more about alternative methods for treating cancer. I'm here to tell you there are so many options and chemo is not the only answer. Pray before you think or even react. God will lead you. Don't just take the doctor's word. Talk to the One who created you. He knows your frame inside and out. He will guide you just as He did me. Don't ever doubt God. He looks for opportunities to prove Himself.

What Does God Say about Healing?

There are some that say if a person is sick and God doesn't heal
them, it means they didn't have enough faith. I've heard people say
that God sends sickness and disease to humble us. There are some
that believe healing isn't available today as it was in the Bible days.
All of these statements are not necessarily true. You may be
wondering where did sickness, disease and death originate other
than in our minds, and were they a part of God's plan? I stand
strongly in my belief that sickness, death and disease were not a part
of God's original plan for us. The opening three chapters of Genesis
clearly show that God's original intent was for perfect people to live
forever on a perfect earth. Everything that God made was *"good"*
there is nothing good about sickness and disease. Now depending on
how tired a person is, or how much they have been through, some
may look at death as being a relief from pain and suffering. But the
beauty of the way things were originally designed, there should
have been no pain or suffering. However, as a result of Adam's sin,
mankind including animals and plants began to suffer, and death
followed.

God created the human body with an amazing, even miraculous
ability to heal itself. In the Old Testament, some verses say that God
sent diseases, plague and etc. However, if you read the passages
more closely, it can be understood as people bringing upon
themselves the consequence of their own sin and unbelief. Every
form of sin has consequences, and the Bible clearly talks about these
consequences. I think about the shoplifter who thinks he has it made
because he successfully stole something without getting caught, or

the woman who had a secret affair with another woman's husband and thought no one knew about it. What about the secretary who stole office supplies and thought no one noticed? I'm pretty sure all of these people felt pretty good about themselves until their sin caught up with them. If people only knew what they were doing to themselves, they would not think themselves to be so clever. So as I stated earlier, sin can bring death, disease and other consequences that you won't see coming. That's why it so important to always be in a place of self-examination and repentance.

My Confessions

My confessions gave me strength; "*I will live and not die and declare the works of the Lord. Lord, you bore my sickness on the cross so that I don't have to bear them. I am whole, complete, and healed by the power of your word. Your word has given me life. I bind every trace of cancer in the name of Jesus. I curse it at the root, never for it to return. Every organ, cyst, lymph node, and tissue is healed. I receive divine healing in Jesus name.*" I repeated this confession over and over, and I believed that by the power of my words and thoughts my healing would eventually come forth.

The time I didn't spend reading, I spent in the kitchen juicing, mixing raw vegetables together, and taking natural supplements and herbs. I would have homemade fruit juice in the morning and a couple of vegetable drinks throughout the rest of the day. I listened to tapes and movies of people who were diagnosed with cancer, and the one thing we didn't have in common was that they claimed the cancer as theirs. I would often hear people say, "*My cancer came* back" "You are snared by the words of your own mouth" (Proverbs 6:2). Have you ever wondered why you can't seem to get well? You could be your biggest problem. I urge you to please watch the words that you speak because it could be those very words that are keeping you bound to sickness. God's Word became my daily bread. Job said; "I have treasured the words of His mouth more than my necessary food" (Job. 23:12). I lived to digest God's truth because in them I found life and hope.

I came across the story of the woman with the issue of blood. This woman's constant hemorrhage was a disaster (Luke 8:43-48). She was left anemic, weak, breathless and hardly able to walk. She was also considered ceremonially unclean, and because of her illness everything and everyone she touched would be considered unclean (Leviticus 15:19-30). One day she heard that Jesus was in town and stopped Him on His way to heal Jarius' daughter. It was her faith and persistence that stopped Jesus in His tracks.

She made her way through the crowd and touched His garment (Luke 8:43). I can hear her saying within herself, "If I could but touch the hem of His garments, I will be made whole." This woman demonstrates how to obtain the healing power of God through faith that produces her healing. What about you? Ask yourself am I exercising my faith to the point, I stop Jesus in His tracks? Are you sitting around feeling sorry for yourself, or are you activating your faith by getting up or out, doing something that can change your situation? Have you gotten to the point of the woman with the issue of blood, saying within yourself, *"I have nothing else to lose. I've got to get to Him. Lord I'm so tired. I don't care who sees me. I'm so broken Lord. I need You Lord; heal me, save me. Lord turn this situation around!"*

After pressing her way through the crowd, she finally made her way to Jesus; at last she touched Him! The Bible says the virtue left His body and instantly she was made whole, and the flow of her blood dried up (Mark. 5:25-35). Her deliverance was in her pressing. No matter what you're going through, you must continue to press; it's during your pressing forward that your faith becomes activated. Notice this woman was on a mission. She didn't just bask in her sickness and hope for a miracle. You never know how close you are to your blessing. So labor, labor long if you have to. Be willing to do whatever it takes, for however long it takes, until your breakthrough comes. You have to be willing to give all you have in everything that you do. If you can't get up, activate the power of your thoughts. Pray continually and tell yourself, *I am healed!*

"But without faith it is impossible to please Him, for he who comes to God must believe that He is, and that He is a rewarder of those that diligently seek Him. "(Hebrew. 11:6). This woman believed that Jesus was able to heal her. God has already established who He is. He says *I AM,* whatever you need Him to be. He already is that and more. It's imperative, if you ever receive a bad report from anyone to always turn to God first, because in Him you will find direction and guidance. *"Call upon Me in the day of trouble; I will deliver you, and you shall glorify Me"* (Psalms 50:15).

God Knows You Best

Think about it: why should we trust doctors just because they wear a white coat and have MD behind their name? It was obvious to me the doctors couldn't help the woman with the issue of blood, If they could have; she wouldn't had a reason to seek out Jesus. She found herself in the same situation the world operates in, which is seeking doctors first instead of seeking the Lord God our healer.

I look at doctors as complete strangers. We take their word for everything. We let them inject us with needles and substances that we have no knowledge about. Could it be that we have more faith in the doctors than we have in God, our healer? I'm not suggesting that you not take any medicine the doctor prescribes, as I do believe some medication is needed at times. I'm simply suggesting everything doesn't require medication. If we deal with the root of any problem, we can prevent the situation from occurring again. Some things require a little more exercise or maybe even changing your eating habits. I truly believe that most of the medicine prescribed to us, doesn't cure us. It seems to only placate the problem. Take my husband for example, he has been on blood pressure medication for years, and he still has high blood pressure.

You would think that since he has been taking two pills every day for three years or so, he would be high blood pressure free by now. But he isn't, because the medication has only regulated his condition, not cured it. I'm only speaking from my own opinion, but if you think about it, you will see some of the same truths in your own life with people you know, or maybe even yourself. *"It's better to trust in God than put confidence in man"* (Psalms 118:8). God has already given us everything we need to heal ourselves with the things of the earth.

Parents stop letting the doctors put your children on so much medication just because they seem a little hyper, eventually they will grow out of it. Back in my younger days, children were just as hyper, but the parents sent them outside to play to exert their high energy. It's a part of the enemies plan to make you think that something is wrong with your child. No, instead pray over them; speak peace, life and prosperity over them, and then send them outside to play.

I remember going to Anderson SC to meet an older caucasian woman. I was referred to her, because she was diagnosed with throat cancer. After getting there and introducing myself, she began to tell me what she had been dealing with. I asked her if she was on any medication. She handed me a Ziploc bag with fifteen different medication bottles in it. This woman had been diagnosed with schizophrenia, cancer, depression, kidney disease and a few others conditions. I remember looking around her home; she had a picture on her wall of her son lying dead in a casket. She was all messed up. The picture on the wall constantly reminded her of the pain of her lost child, thus causing her so much sadness, depression and grief. The doctors had prescribed her so much medication to treat her condition that the side effects of the medications were making her delusional. She literally didn't know if she was coming or going.

I tried talking with her, and praying with her, and even asked her about removing those photos on her wall. Nothing seemed to help. I left her house feeling sad for her. I did all I could. She had been living in that condition for years. Unless Jesus Himself physically came down and stepped in, I didn't see any hope for her.

It's very important that you shift mentally and understand that everything starts and ends with God, not with man. Man doesn't have all the answers. To overcome and reverse any illness or situation, it takes the power of God to deliver you and faith that is a flowing brook. That means your faith has to go beyond where you are, and you must not doubt that nothing is too hard for God. The leper was sure Jesus was more than capable of healing him, but he wasn't sure if it was His will. He asked Jesus, *"Lord, if You are willing You can make me clean, and Jesus, moved with compassion, put forth His hand and touched him, and said unto him, I am willing, be thou clean"* (Mark. 1:40, 41). You must believe the same for yourself also; believe that He is willing.

The promises of God says, *"above all, I wish that thou mayest prosper and be in health even as thy soul prospers"* (3 John 1:2). This Scripture, along with plenty others, clearly states that God intends for us to have good health and prosperity. Sickness is demonic. It's of the devil, and we don't have to accept it into our lives. You read in a previous chapter where I talked about sin and its consequences. *"If you diligently heed the voice of the Lord your God, and do what is right in His sight, give ear to His commandments and keep all His statues, I will put none of the diseases on you which I have brought on the Egyptians; for I am the Lord who heals you"* (Exod. 15:26). I have come to learn that we are not our own. We have been bought at a high price. We belong to God, and that means obeying His commandments and statutes; otherwise the consequences can be detrimental. So right now, if you are sick or going through anything major in your life, repent if you know you have un-confessed sin in your life.

Chapter Nine

It's Working for Your Good

The footnote in the Open New King James Study Bible says; God allows suffering for different reasons. Sometimes it's a situation like Job's, which is to prove to the enemy you will serve God no matter what. Other times, it could be a situation we have brought on ourselves. It doesn't matter what we go through because, *"And we know that all things work together for good to those who love God, to those who are the called according to His purpose"* (Romans 8:28). This passage is addressed to those who love God. According to this scripture, ALL THINGS, everything that has happened, is happening, or will happen works for your good. Nothing in your life is accidental. We as Christians need to consider our present condition or situation in the light of our assurance about the future. We don't always understand or see the purposes of God. But the promise of God guarantees *"good"* for His children. So even if you don't understand why you're going through what you're going through, trust God and know it's all working together for your good.

Your Passion

Your passion is produced from your pain. I always thought that my passion was working with teenage girls, whom I still love, but a new passion has been birthed in me.

I am now more passionate about educating people about this intruder called cancer. Far too many people are dying because they trusted in everything except the promises of God. When you feel something is going on in your body that's not normal, don't hesitate to seek medical attention. God's purpose for our lives has already been established before the foundations of the world. What you're going through right now may have caught you off guard, but there are no surprises with God. Even if it's something we have caused ourselves, our God is still faithful and stands ready to deliver us.

As I chose to trust God, I knew that it was a process I would have to go through. I often thought about the people whose lives would be affected by my faith walk. My husband was the closest to me, and I knew that he was watching. I gained power to keep going the more I fell to my knees in prayer.

However, the enemy wasn't letting up. It seems like the stronger I got, the weaker I became. God gave me a revelation: "*He that is in you is greater than he that is in the world*" (1John 4:4). I realized that since the greatness of God dwells in me, and God is all powerful, then the power of God and sickness can't reside in the same temple. The power of God would rise up in me, and I would put the devil under my feet where he belonged.

I would continue to bind Satan and his demons and loose God's healing power in my life. "*Whatever you bind on earth will be bound in heaven and whatever you loose on earth will be loosed in heaven*" (Matthew 6:19). I was willing to do whatever it took to get well. I knew that death and life was in the power of the tongue, and that we have the power to create our world just as God did in the beginning. The same power that God has, when He said "*Let there be*" is the same power He gave us. "*Let there be complete and divine healing."* I decided that I wanted my world to be full of good health and prosperity just as God desires for us. I had to bind my own thoughts at times, as well as any negative behavior I got from other people. I really had to spend time loosing God's protection over me, and asking Him to cover me in His blood. I felt extremely safe under the blood. Please, I urge you to constantly plead the blood of Jesus over your life, because there are demonic forces working in the unseen realm of the spirit that are sent and assigned to destroy you.

My Friend and Mentor

By this point, I had a pretty good idea of what I was dealing with and everything it was going to take to be healed. The Lord is so good. He sent me someone who would be a long term friend, as well as mentor. One day, my husband and I were in the grocery store and came across a lady that we knew in business. This woman had a brother that had been suffering from insomnia. She began to tell us about a woman named Terry Hall who helped her brother get better. She said this woman owned a store in downtown Greenville and specialized in natural foods and holistic medicines. I was open to speaking with her as I was still interested in learning more about how to get rid of the cancer from a holistic standpoint. I took down her number and set up an appointment to meet with her. My meeting with Terry opened my eyes even more. She began to guide me and show me other alternatives that could be used to get rid of cancer. This woman was truly God sent. God used her not only to help me through cancer, but He used her to help me with the emotions that would follow. She literally became my nutritionist, counselor and friend.

If you or a loved one has been diagnosed with cancer, I think you owe it to yourself and to them, to find out as much information about this disease as possible. So many people to this day are still ignorant as to the causes of cancer. Now of course no one knows everything, but whatever the situation is do your own research. The more knowledgeable you are about it, the more confident you will feel that you can overcome it. Knowledge, application, and faith can change any situation.

Do Your Own Research

75% of people who have been diagnosed with cancer opt to take the treatments. There are tons of statistics and proof that shows conventional cancer treatments are unsuccessful, poisonous and life threatening. Then you have some patients that want the cancer gone so desperately, they choose every option available including surgery, chemo and radiation, as well as the use of alternative medicines. Oncologist's strongly suggest and promote the use of taking treatments because the truth is, for nearly 40 years, the United States has spent over $200 billion trying to find a cure without any success.

The average conventional cancer treatment costs around $50,000 per patient, but most natural cancer remedies and cures cost less than a thousand dollars. It doesn't matter what type of cancer it is or what stage the cancer is in, their method of treatment is all the same. There are different drugs for different types of cancer, but none of them guarantee your healing. It's like playing Russian roulette with your life. I understand that some things aren't certain, but the treatments that the oncologist offers have way too many side effects. It's just too risky. It seems there have been more people who have died from the treatments, than there is who have lived because of them. It's strange that we never hear about the people who have died because of the treatments, you only hear about the 3% of people who survived, which usually are the ones who have gone into remission and it's been 10, 15, 20 years later. However, chemotherapy does not work for 97% of people, but using the more natural approach the survival rate is 90%.

Now please keep in mind, this is my book and some of these statements are based on my opinion, but the percentages and other facts are based on my extensive research concerning cancer. I can assure you the pharmaceutical industry has a vested interest in cancer treatments due to the large amount of money the industry makes off of patients who take the treatments. Three months to a year is all it should take to turn any situation around concerning your health. This will require discipline, faith and a complete life style change.

During a seminar for Nature's Sunshine in Asheville N.C., I sat through a class as the digestive system was being discussed. During the seminar, I learned that herbs change the environment of the body so it can begin to heal itself. If we stop feeding our bodies the bad foods, the disease will leave. Think about this for a moment, rats won't live in a clean home. If your home is clean and in order, there's no food on the floor, or all over the counter then you won't have a problem with rodents. It's the same with our body. Stop putting bad things in your body and you cut down on the risk of disease.

Love and Fear

Another factor that plays a huge part in sickness is our emotions. There are only two basic emotions that we all experience: love and fear; all other emotions are variations of these. Thoughts and behaviors come from either a place of love or a place of fear. The emotions of anxiety, anger, control, sadness, depression, inadequacy, confusion, hurt, loneliness, guilt, and shame are all fear-based emotions. Emotions such as joy, happiness, caring, trust, compassion, truth, contentment, and satisfaction are all love-based emotions.

When we are experiencing fear, it damages the immune system, the endocrine system, and every other vital system in our bodies. Fear weakens our immune system, and opens the door for serious illnesses to come in. Depression and chronic stress are the two most common emotions associated with cancer. When you are in love, your body releases special chemicals that make you feel strong, content, happy and able to conquer the world. It's sad to say, but we often let our emotions get the best of us.

We must be conscious of our emotional state at all times and look for ways to unwind. When I'm worked up or stressed, I quickly escape to the park. Whatever I'm dealing with, I've learned I can take it to the park and leave it there; something about being around nature helps me to unwind. It's where I can get physical exercise and pray about any situation at hand. I've also recently started doing guided meditations. I find this to be the best form of stress relief for me. What does this look like for me? Well, I go to YouTube and choose a video dealing with stress and health. I then comfortably lay flat on my bed away from all noise and distractions, while a soothing and gentle voice guides me into a place of peace and relaxation. I may lay there for ten minutes to an hour. When I've completed my meditation, I usually feel completely relaxed and very calm. I can be in a situation of complete turmoil and not be affected by it.

I usually do meditations several times a month. When my husband has a lot on his mind, or is stressed he finds comfort in golfing. My advice is to find what works for you, because we all need an outlet to remove stress.

What You Don't Know Can Hurt You

There is an old cliché, "What you don't know can't hurt you." Well I'm here to tell you, what you don't know can hurt you, and even kill you. Fran Drescher, as she battled uterine cancer, wrote something in her book "Cancer Schmancer", that was an eye opener for me: *"We are the ones who must change, if we expect there to be change."* We must take control of the situation and become educated people. Know your body and always be aware of your emotional state as well as keeping your stress level low. Spend time getting to know God. It's when you understand and know who He is, you find out who you are. God is peace in the midst of a storm and you can handle anything that comes your way, because of Him.

Cancer Facts

The two avenues that cancer enters the body are through the fluid system, which involve the lymphatic system, and the blood system. No one is exempt from cancer. As a matter of fact, we all have cancer cells growing in our bodies every day, but not everyone will develop cancer. One of the major differences between someone who has cancer and someone who doesn't is the diagnosed person's immune system wasn't able to fight off the disease, and therefore cancer developed. That is precisely why I began to take a lot of supplements and eat foods that targeted my immune system. I knew that if I could strengthen my immune system, in addition to eating right and ensuring I remained in a healthy emotional state, I had a good chance of reversing the cancer. It wasn't hard. In fact, I believe it kept me from feeling the symptoms from the cancer. If you are a person who has never considered herbs, look into them. There are so many that target and promote a healthy immune system.

I started looking over a list of the chemotherapy drugs the oncologist gave me and for every drug listed, there was a long list of side effects. This puzzled me, how could a medicine that is designed to make you get well, have so many dangerous side effects? I was also given a book entitled *"Eating Hints for Cancer Patients."* It discussed complementary medicines, which are natural herbs and supplements. It says this medicine given for cancer has not been proven safe, and if one spent time taking complementary medicines, which is herbs and supplements, one may lose valuable treatment time and reduce one's chances of controlling the cancer and getting well. Based upon my research, I haven't read any stories indicating that natural medicines have caused any serious life threatening side effects, in fact just the opposite. However, there are many horror stories concerning those who took the standard treatments.

The oncologist may put pressure on you to make a decision regarding traditional treatment because time is of the essence, but I suggest you take time with your decision as it will likely be one that will change your life forever. I didn't care what the doctors thought or said. I needed to pray and allow God to lead me. I'm so thankful that I had a mind to seek Him. I believed that God was my healer, and I refused to let go of Him until my healing came forth. I couldn't imagine my healing coming from something that could make me worse than I already was. It really didn't make sense to me.

How can something that is supposed to make you well turn out to be so deadly? Why is it legal for doctors to administer it? The doctor I had never educated me on the infection in my body, which later turned out to be Hodgkin's Disease/cancer. All he told me was, there was an infection, it was in my lymph nodes, and they weren't certain of the cause.

God's Medicine

"And God said, See I have given you every herb that yields seed which is on the face of all the earth, and every tree whose fruit yields seeds: to you it shall be for food" (Genesis 1:29). Even though there are many different causes and types of cancer, there's still no reason to be afraid. Believe it or not, your healing is already at your disposal. God has given us our food and in our food are all the nutrients the body needs to maintain good health. Think about it. When a dog is sick, he begins to eat grass. When humans get sick, why do we turn to chicken noodle soup and immediately run to physicians? We should turn to the foods of

the earth such as leafy greens and vegetables, as well as fruit. We should also be taking some form of multivitamin and herbs to boost the immune system.

When Adam and Eve were in the Garden of Eden, their food consisted of the food of the earth. *"He causes the grass to grow for the cattle, and vegetation for the service of man, that he may bring forth food from the earth." (Ps.* 104: 14). Everything that God created, He called *good* including our food. There was nothing polluted about it, at least not then. It's not even safe to go to the grocery store and buy anything off the shelves these days.

Families are eating processed foods and meats loaded with hormones and chemicals. This could be perceived as a harsh statement, but this is only my opinion. I genuinely feel that because of the foods women and men buy and cook for their families they could be putting their families in harm's way without even realizing it. These processed foods, and foods filled with hormones and chemicals, create an environment in our bodies that allows disease to rear its ugly head. Parents, spend some extra time in the grocery stores reading the ingredients of the foods you purchase. Stay tuned, you will learn more at the end of the book about certain ingredients to watch out for.

Chapter Ten

Faith Verses Fear

I learned that God's perfect will is not to heal us; His perfect will is for us not to get sick. (Isiah 38:1-5) tells the story of Hezekiah the king. Hezekiah was sick unto death. The prophet came and said, *'Boy, you're going to die."* He could have cursed God, and had a pity party. He could have easily begun to live it up, especially since he knew he was going to die. Instead, he prayed and asked God for extended life and because of his prayer God extended his life fifteen years, *"yet ye have not, because ye ask not"* (James 4:2). He is the same God; you have nothing to lose by asking God for extended life. It worked for Hezekiah.

Speak to your Situation

It is very important that you develop a habit of speaking healing to your body. I do this on a regular basis. I can be riding in my car and I'm constantly speaking divine healing and wholeness to every cyst, organ, tissue, and cell. I curse disease at its roots. What you think and declare is your own responsibility. The more you fill your mind and spirit with the word of God, the easier it is to overcome those ungodly thinking patterns.

Everything you desire, whether it is good health, bills paid, peace of mind, a promotion on your job, husband or wife saved, whatever the situation may be, let it be unto you according to your faith. Faith and fear can't operate in the same situation. Either you are fearful, or you will have enough faith to believe. Fear causes much torment, while faith causes you to have peace. If you find yourself always worried and reasoning within yourself, then it's a good chance you have let fear get the best of you. Doubt and fear is a sneaky thing because so many of us operate in it without realizing it. We are up at night walking the floors, stressed out, depressed, and feeling defeated. Most of the time we don't realize these emotions until sickness is present or someone brings them to our attention.

I had the privilege of being used by God to minister to other women and men who were battling cancer. I had come to believe that if God led me to a person who was sick, He wanted to heal them. I talked with countless people who had already adopted a defeated mindset. Most of them had been diagnosed with cancer in prior years, and the cancer had returned. I surrendered myself and allowed God to use me, and share my story about faith in God and trusting in Him for my healing. I spoke of natural supplements and diet changes, but it amazed me how just about every one of them hung onto the doctor's reports. Who will stand up and believe the report of the Lord? It's not my job to persuade or influence anyone to do as I did. I can only share my faith.

I heard Dr. Mike Murdock a spiritual leader that teaches on wisdom say something that was so profound. He said, *"It's our faith that decides God's divine timing in our life."* That really ministered to me because so many times we say, *"It's all in God's time,"* and I do believe that everything is according to His divine timing. It also means, the sooner you act in faith and believe God for your miracle, the sooner your miracle comes forth. For example, if you believe God for a new job, it's one thing to pray and ask for it, but it's another thing to believe in faith, and begin to thank God for the job before you even have it. It's possible your faith in Him causes Him to move faster on your behalf.

A Wonderful Encounter

There is a Methodist church down the street from my home. I have noticed at least once a month there is a sign posted on the marquee out front that says, *"Healing service tonight 7:00 p.m.* One day in particular around 6:15 that evening, I rode past the church and saw the sign. I immediately told myself that I was going, and had 45 minutes to get myself together and get back to the service by seven. By the time I'd gotten home, I had quickly talked myself out of going. While I was in the kitchen, a pain went through my stomach, and I fell to the floor! *"Okay Lord, I hear you"* I said to myself. I hurried and gathered my things and left the house. When I arrived I was the only African American in the church, and everyone was much older than me.

I had never been to a church like that before, and I'd also never felt the love of God like I had experienced there. We sang songs, had communion, and there were prayer requests being offered up. Then they asked everyone to come to the altar and kneel in prayer. What really touched me was they had elders and prayer warriors at the front of the church. The person leading the service asked if anyone would like to come up front to receive prayer. I accepted this call and went up front. There were two women and one man standing with me. One lady immediately asked me, *"What is your favorite color?"* I told her *"green"* at least that's what I thought it was at the time. Anyway, there was a lady in the back of the church making quilted blankets and I was instructed to walk to the back and pick out one. As I returned with the blanket, one of the women took the blanket from my hand and began to wrap it around me.

She said to me, *"Anytime you feel afraid, or need to feel the presence and the peace of God, wrap yourself in this blanket."* They asked me what my prayer request was. I told them, *"The doctors told me I had cancer, and I believe God is going to heal me without chemo and radiation."* They stood in agreement with me and began to pray for me one by one. As I stood there in the middle of them, I could only cry as I felt the presence of the Lord in me and all around me. The prayers were so sweet and the people were so genuine. That experience was one I will never forget. I left the church feeling very encouraged, and even more motivated to stop at nothing to obtain divine health. I believed that whatever God was going to do in me, He was already doing. I continued to walk in faith, believing that God was with me every step of the way.

I heard Apostle Ron Carpenter, a well-known pastor from Greenville S.C say, *"If God was going to do anything in the earth, He would work through people."* God is spirit and His spirit needs a body to work through. Can God trust you to work through?

Why aren't there more services about healing? I realized this was much needed. Could it be we don't have the faith to believe that God can work through us? I thought at one point, just because my healing hadn't yet been manifested, I couldn't lay hands on anyone, but I was so wrong. It seemed God really began to use me while I believed Him for my own healing.

In the name of Jesus

There is power in the name of Jesus. If you haven't tried using His name, try it. Use it with faith and assurance. Declare and decree that cancer, or whatever your issue maybe has to bow down to His name. You may have to say it over and over at times. Do this along with the other things that are suggested to bring forth your healing or a change in your situation. God told Moses to use what he had in his hand. Moses had everything he needed to perform the task at hand. We too have everything we need; we just have to realize that we already have it. Open up your mouth and bless God! Stop moping around in your situation. You never know your healing, or deliverance could be in your praise. Either way, God is waiting on you, while you think you're waiting on Him.

Don't get so involved in spiritual warfare that your attention is on the devil more than it is on God. *"As they set out, Jehosophat stood and said, listen to me, Judah and people of Jerusalem! Have faith in the Lord your God and you will be upheld; have faith in His prophets and you will be successful".* After consulting with the people, Jehoshaphat appointed men to sing to the Lord and to praise Him for the splendor of His holiness as they went out at the head of the army, saying; *"Give thanks to the Lord for His love endures forever."* As they began to sing and praise, the Lord set ambushes against the men of Ammon and Moab and Mount Seir who were invading Judah, and they were defeated (2Chronicles 20:20-22). You are literally going to battle with evil forces, you have to know you have the victory before you go, and understand the battle is not yours, but the Lord's. So be encouraged and take your stand. Take back what the enemy is trying to steal from you. No matter the situation, you ARE victorious! Open your mouth and give God the greatest praise you have ever given Him! Keep praising Him until the enemy of sickness and death is destroyed in your life.

Chapter Eleven

Spiritual Weapons

The weapons the Lord has given us are not carnal, they are spiritual. As a matter of fact everything is spiritual, *"For the weapons of our warfare are not carnal but mighty through God to the pulling down of strongholds"* (2 Corinthians 10:4).

Here we stand in the midst of a fallen world, while the spiritual battle rages all around. Satan and his fallen angels work night and day to keep us living in a broken and defeated state so that we don't advance the kingdom of God (2 Corinthians 4:3-4). The battle is over the souls of humanity. Satan works to keep God's people ignorant, blind, and sick, thus making us completely unware of his devices. Take a stand against the enemy and declare no more concerning your situation and walk in victory. Stop fighting with carnal weapons and use the word of God.

Understand that Satan is your enemy. He doesn't like you and doesn't have your best interest at heart. When you are blind to this fact, he has you right where he wants you. Put the devil on the run; kick him out of your situation, and speak words that will change your life.

When Jesus cursed the fig tree, the leaves didn't wither immediately. He spoke the words, and later what He spoke began to manifest. I said that to say, you may be declaring God's Word and speaking it over and over, but your healing hasn't manifested. Please don't stop your declarations and please don't stop believing that you have your healing, or whatever you're asking God for. It is done! You must continue to wait on the manifestation and remember to neglect how you may be feeling while you're waiting. Your circumstance may still look the same, but keep trusting and waiting on God. God's Word is true. If He said it, then it is so! *"Heaven and earth will pass away, but My Word will stand forever"* (Isaiah 40:8). My greatest struggle was dealing with cancer and I had to keep myself encouraged. You will in fact have to do the same. There may not be people around you to encourage you, especially when you need it the most.

Your Perception

Things are not always what they seem to be. The way people view you and the way you present yourself is the impression you leave behind. If you are driving around in a Bentley, dressed in a three piece suit, with stacks of money and wearing a Rolex. People are going to automatically assume that you are very wealthy or a drug dealer. When in reality, that car could be a rental. The watch could be a fake, and that stack of money could have a $20 bill on top and 50 one dollar bills underneath, giving the illusion of a wealthy person or someone who looks like he sells drugs.

I read a quote that says; *"When the truth is blurred by lies and misinformation, perception becomes reality and all is lost.* "Don't create a false perception to fake people out because the only one you are really fooling is yourself. The truth about cancer and the conventional treatments have been concealed by lies and misinformation. Therefore mankind suffers a great loss, just as one would as he goes around trying to fool people.

If you don't like the way that your life is playing out you can always take charge of your own perception of reality. You are in control of your story. I challenge you to change the way you view your current situation. Have faith in God and live. What do you have to lose by believing the situation that you're in, is not unto death?

What's your perception of who Jesus is? Do you perceive Him to be the Son of man or the Son of God? If you perceive Him to be the Son of man, then you see Him as being Joseph's son. You believe there is nothing powerful about Him. If you believe Him to be the Son of God, then you know Him to be the Messiah. He stands ready and able to deliver you. However you see Him, is how He will show up on your behalf. Do you see Him as a healer? If so then He is that and more. If you see Him as your Provider, then everything that you need has already been taken care of. Your perception creates your reality.

I chose life

"I call heaven and earth as witnesses today against you, that I have set before you life and death, blessing and cursing; therefore choose life, that both you and your descendants may live; that you may love the Lord your God, that you may obey His voice, and that you may cling to Him, for His is your life" (Deuteronomy 30:19-20). These words come from some of the last words that God gave Moses to write just before his death. Choosing life first means to love God and walk in His ways. Adam and Eve were given a choice to obey God, or do as they pleased. They chose to disobey God and to this

very day we are still reaping the consequences of their choice. To obey is the essence of the Christian faith. Jesus was *"obedient unto death, even the death on the cross"* (Philippians 2:8). The bible also makes it very clear that we should show our love for Jesus by obeying Him in all things, *"If you love Me, Keep My commandments"* (John 14:15). To choose their own way meant rebellion, death and curses. *"For the wages of sin is death, but the gift of God is eternal life in Christ Jesus our Lord"* (Romans 6:23).

Choosing life also means standing firm in your decision to live a Godly life, loving and accepting Christ as your Savior. It's overcoming whatever that has you bound. There's something about making a decision. God gave us the freedom to choose. So many times things happen to us, and we allow them because we are indecisive about what we want to do, or which direction we should take. You have the power and the ability to choose your outcome. I choose not to accept sickness. I have a shirt that says, *"I choose life."* I literally had to make a conscious decision to live, and so will you.

"And if it seems evil unto you to serve the Lord, Choose ye this day whom ye will serve, but as for me and my house, we will serve the Lord" (Joshua 24:15). It's all about what you choose, decide and accept. God doesn't force anything on you. Have you chosen Christ as your Lord? That should be the first decision any of us makes. It's certainly the most important decision of your life.

It brought me great peace to know that God was present with me every step of the way. I knew He had my back, however the situation turned out. The Bible talks about being sober. The enemy knows if he can catch you sleeping, he can throw anything your way. If he can keep your mind racing going back and forth, never making a decision, he knows he can slip confusion into your mind. There's an old saying, *"if you don't stand for something, you will fall for anything."* So what do you choose? Do you choose life or death, sickness or poverty? If you don't make a decision, you have already chosen without being aware of it.

I decided to go with life more abundantly, so I had to continue standing and trusting in God. I had to stand trusting Him, or die believing Him. Chemo and radiation were not an option. At one point my mind began to play tricks on me. In my imagination, I saw myself as if I had died. Honestly, at one point I entertained the thoughts of suicide, but they weren't my thoughts they were of the enemy. I had to catch myself, and for the first time I begin to think about what I was thinking about. I remembered that I was choosing life and that certainly didn't involve death. Living was my only option.

I hadn't even been married a year at that time, and my husband and I had so much that we wanted to do. We had a trip to San Diego California planned for August. I was determined I was going, and going cancer free at that.

Chapter Twelve

No Pain, No Glory

My brother gave me a CD from a revival at a church he attended. The title of the message was "*No Pain, No Glory.*" The title alone ministered to me. If I was going to be used by God, I would have to endure some pain and suffering. I told God if this is the cup that I have to drink, I will drink it. After all, Jesus had to do the same thing. People kept telling me, "*God is going to use you to minister to other people in the same situation.*" I always have a ready mind to tell others about the goodness of Jesus, so I accepted the fact that my pain would become my ministry. I remember going to my sister's wedding and driving to Florida. On the way back my family and I found ourselves in the midst of Hurricane Katrina that took place in September 2005. A storm came from out of nowhere and it started to pour rain. While driving, I had gotten to a point where I could no longer see the road. I saw people with their blinkers on driving slowly, while others had stopped completely because they couldn't see. The rain was coming down hard.

Even though cancer was my storm, I couldn't stop. At times, I was like those drivers that couldn't see. I could have pulled over, meaning to give up, feel hopeless, defeated, and accept the doctor's report. I chose to put my blinkers on, take it a bit slower and drive through the storm.

This was the season that I was in however; I don't believe a Christian's life is one of continual storms. Some Christians believe that if they aren't suffering or going through something awful, then something must be wrong with their relationship with God. Yes it's true, *"If we suffer with Him, we will reign with Him"* (2 Timothy 2:12). So there will be some times of suffering, along with times of peace and happiness. But when you have complete joy in the Lord, you won't even look at your storms as being storms. You begin to see them as opportunities to share Christ goodness.

We are all going to leave this earth someday. Yes, Jesus defeated death on the cross. That means if you are a Christian our bodies will one day return to the dust of the earth, but our spirits will live on forever with our Father in Heaven.

I wouldn't trade this experience for anything in the world. God is faithful. If He brings you to it, He will bring you through it. Our life is a journey and we are constantly changing and growing. I encourage you to keep walking, praying, and continue believing. You're not going anywhere until God's appointed time and you are certainly not alone. God, through Jesus is affiliated with your pain. He knows exactly how you feel and stands ready to deliver you.

Abram's Faith

It is always my desire to please God by my acts of faith. *"And he believed in the Lord, and He was accounted it to him for righteousness* (Genesis15:6). When Abram was asked to offer his only son Isaac up for a sacrifice, God was pleased with his faith. God provided a ram to be offered up instead. (Genesis 22:1-14). It was only a test. What you're going through right now could be a test. Are you passing or failing? Do you believe God is pleased with how you are handling the situation you may be facing, or do you find yourself complaining? I found out very quickly that complaining doesn't help any situation get better it only makes things worse.

There wasn't anything that I did so great that God would show me His favor. We can't earn righteousness by our good works. God loves us in spite of what we do, or don't do. However, you can please God by having steadfast faith in Him. Think about it, what else do you have to lose? Some people are extremely wealthy, but when it comes down to it, our money doesn't earn us any extra rewards. If you're fortunate enough to live a long life, you certainly can't take money with you. Have faith and turn to God. Ask Him to show you how to take care of yourself and to always be mindful of the things that really matter.

You only have one body here on earth. You only have one chance to make a difference and get it right. Whatever you have to do to be in right standing with God, do it and move forward. God wants to bless you and deliver you. Repent as often as we need to. God loves us so much; He stands ready to forgive us if we are sincere. God wants to take your pain and turn it into your message.

The Meaning of Pain

Pain is a signal that something is wrong and needs to be fixed. If you think about it, it's a sign of God's love. It tells us when something is wrong, and sometimes it protects us from more harm. However, I have learned that God allowed the pain in my body to remind me that there has been a diagnosis. Paul writes; "*And because of the surpassing greatness of the revelations, for this reason to keep me from exalting myself, there was given a thorn in the flesh, a messenger of Satan to buffet me, to keep me from exalting myself"*(2 Corinthians 12:7). Paul begged the Lord three times concerning his throne; The Lord said to Paul, *"My grace is sufficient for you, for My strength is made perfect in weakness"*(2 Corinthians12:9). *Therefore I take pleasure in infirmities, in reproaches, in needs, in persecutions, in distresses, for Christ's sake. For when I am weak, then I am strong"* (2 Corinthians 12:10).

That truly is the power of God and the mindset that you must have. How many of us actually boast in our weakness, or pain? Not many that I have come across. Most of us sit around and complain and want people to feel sorry for us. The meat of Paul's message is saying God's grace is sufficient for you regardless of the situation. We live each day in God's grace, and it's by grace that we are able to stand. His grace refers to divine favor, to divine blessings, and to divine benefits. It refers to that which God has given us in Christ, not because we earned it or deserved it, but because He willed to give it. All of God's gifts are given to His children by grace.

It was truly God's grace that helped me deal with cancer. I get so humbled when I think about how many people died from cancer, but God saw fit and spared my life. I give Him all the glory, honor and praise. He was there before I uttered His name. God is always near and always present. There will sometimes be poverty, sickness, and death. He allows things to happen for different reasons. He doesn't always intervene and block things from happening, but He promises to be there when you call Him. It's a part of life and even in the midst of your troubles; God is still good and still faithful.

We serve a God who doesn't sleep or slumber, so why should we lie awake at night worrying about something that ultimately God has control over? I chose victory over defeat, and I knew that my life was in the Master's hand. Victory only comes through battle, and triumph follows trials. To me, victory was living through it all and being able to help and see someone else through. It's called paying it forward. That's how we begin to spread the love and the power of God. We begin to change one life at a time.

What makes me victorious is my mindset and coming out of my experience with a closer relationship with God and my family. That would be the sweet taste of victory for me. What does victory look like to you? Whatever it looks like, declare that and don't waiver from it.

Chapter Thirteen

There Is a Cure

There is only one true way to successfully treat cancer and other forms of disease and that is through the use of a whole body approach. While studying and researching things that I could do to get well, I learned that I must treat my whole body. You cannot drug a body into good health. You must nourish the body, mind and soul. Cancer is a systemic disorder, which means it is the whole body. It simply manifests itself in a particular organ or site.

I am very aware of the fact that most people didn't know there was a cure for cancer. Everywhere you turn, you see advertisements about raising money for the cure. There are organizations all over the world that are raising money for cancer. I'm always so bothered by these initiatives because there is certainly a cure for cancer, just as there are for conditions like HIV/AIDS. As I stated earlier, there's a 90% cure rate with the use of herbs and a whole body approach. The side effects are minimal to none. I never experienced any side effects, and at one point I was taking up to 30 herbs a day.

Herbal treatments are being used that do not damage healthy cells, because they target cancer cells only and either gently kill the cancer cells, or revert them into normal cells. Thus the herbs and supplements can be used in very high doses plus in many cases several of these treatments can be combined for an even greater effect. While on my mission to reverse the cancer, IP6 with Inositol, Essiac Tea as well as Vitamin B17 was the treatment options that I used and found to have excellent results. These inexpensive safe and gentle cancer treatments have existed for decades, but very few people know of these treatments. I love introducing vitamins and herbs to people and watch the amazement in their eyes as I tell them there is a cure.

One Powerful Cure

It would be remiss if I didn't share a little more information about the powerful tea I just mentioned. Rene Caisse, a Canadian Nurse back in 1922, met a woman who claimed to have been cured of advanced breast cancer. This woman credited her cure to an ancient Native Indian recipe of herbs and roots given to her 30 years previously by an Ontario Indian medicine man. Caisse asked the elderly lady to reveal which herbs were used, also how and when to take them. This potent information was filed away for a couple years.

Later Caisse's aunt was diagnosed with cancer of the stomach and liver and was considered to be terminal. Caisse remembered the secret cure she had been told about years earlier, and decided to try them on her aunt. Her aunt's doctor, Dr. R.O Fisher agreed and allowed Caisse to try the new brew. She dug up the recipe to the tea, brewed it, and treated her aunt successfully. She lived another 21 years with no recurrence.

Convinced of the tea's ability to cure cancer, Caisse refined and tested the remedy beginning what would be a life-long quest for its acceptance in the medical world for the treatment of cancer. Caisse who died at the age of 90 believed wholeheartedly in her formula and wanted desperately to help those sick with cancer. She left her mark on the world of medicine as we know it. In fact her last name spelled backwards is the name of this powerful tea, Essiac.

Essiac consists of four main herbs that grow in the wilderness of Ontario, Canada. The four main herbs that make up Essiac are: Burdock Root, Slippery Elm Inner Bark, Sheep Sorrel, and Indian Rhubarb Root. This tea is also useful in detoxification and immune system strengthening.

In the powerful words of Renee Caisse

"I have never claimed that my treatment cures cancer-although many of my patients, and doctors with whom I have worked with claim that it does. My goal has been control of cancer, and alleviation of pain."

I had already discovered the tea through researching online. The more I read about it, the more I became intrigued. It was absolutely fascinating. The reviews were great and there were tons of testimonials from those who had drunk the tea and it reversed their cancer. I came across one testimonial from a lady that lives in Florida. She had been battling liver cancer for years, someone introduced the tea to her and she started to drink it. She was so confident about the tea; she posted her phone number and said that she would be willing to confirm the great benefits of the tea if anyone called her about it.

I decided to call. Her name was Ms. Evans; she was open and very straight forward. She began to tell me all that she had been going through concerning cancer. I asked her about the tea, she confirmed that Essiac Tea is a very powerful tea. She said she had been drinking it six months and all the cancer was gone. She didn't want to do chemotherapy because she was too old, and didn't want to spend the rest of her days being sick from the side effects of the treatments. Ms. Evans would have her daughter come and fix the tea for her and drank it faithfully. She highly recommended that I drank the tea and told me I would not be disappointed. She never spoke of any side effects concerning the tea, and asked me to keep in touch. From that point on, Essiac Tea was at the top of my list. There are hundreds of reviews about the powerful effects of this tea. I would recommend this tea to anyone dealing with cancer.

Growing Up

My childhood consisted of me not being allowed to be sick. As I mentioned earlier in the book, my mother was a nurse and being sick wasn't an option in my home. Because my mind was trained from a very early age, it made it easier for my subconscious mind to line up with my conscious thoughts, that I can't be sick.

Where You Come From

Question for you, what was your childhood like? Did you grow up in a negative environment where you saw defeat, sickness and poverty? Did you see your parents consistently struggling and often claiming sickness? You've been trying to figure out why you are the way that you are, but the truth is we are what we come from. In order to undo this generational curse, you must first recognize the negative affect it may have on you, and make a conscious decision to change, doing the exact opposite of what you grew up witnessing.

"Watch your thoughts, for they become words. Choose your words, for they become actions. Understand your actions, for they become habits. Study your habits, for they will become your character. Develop your character, for it becomes your destiny." Anonymous

I remember one night talking with Christina, a waitress at the Waffle House, before she began her shift I would ask her with much excitement in my voice, *"Are you going to make a lot of money today?" She* had been complaining of financial hardship and needed to make some money. She told me, *"No, second shift doesn't make any money, so I won't make any money today."* Her attitude before she hit the clock was negative. She thought just because she was working a slow shift that it was impossible to make money. I told her, *"If you don't think you're going to make money, then you won't. Change your thoughts, believe every need is met and what you need to make in this day, you will make."*

After having this conversation with her about three different times, she finally got it. Later, I saw Christina and she was so excited. I asked her once again, had she been making money and she lit up with excitement and told me, *yes!* Things were changing for her, and of course she was glad to finally be making money to change her situation. It's really that simple, there's power in your belief. Whatever you whole heartily believe, will happen for you.

Concerning your Health

Many people decide to take treatments, and that's one's own personal choice. I'm not here to convince or persuade anyone to do as I did; it's according to your own faith. Whatever you decide to do, believe and know why you are doing it. Don't just do something because everyone thinks you should. Have your own reason, and 100% faith in what you are doing. It doesn't matter if you're going to college, believe that when you finish, you will get a good job. If you're applying for a job or buying a home; believe that you already have it. People around you may doubt, but don't you be the one that doubt. Believe that it's yours. My husband says, *"You can have it, go get it!*

How I stayed encouraged

Pastor Roberts and his wife Lindsey sent me a CD with nothing but Scripture on it. Their instructions were to listen to it over and over until the Word got down in my spirit. The more I heard the Word, the stronger my faith became. God allowed me to meet up with people of great faith to lay hands on me and anoint me. As I look back I could see how everything was strategically set up by God. God gave me songs that kept me encouraged. *"To be Kept by Jesus"* by Juanita Bynum, *"Jesus"* by Shekinah Glory, *"Resting on His Promises"* by Youthful Praise, and *"All I need"* by Brian Courtney Wilson were all songs that God used to minister to me. Music and sound also have the power to heal the body, mind and spirit. There is a famous quote by Khalil Gibran that says, *"Music is the language of the spirit. It opens the secret of life bringing peace, and abolishing strife"* I would also add healing.

God is saying, *"Be strong and of good courage, do not fear nor be afraid of them; for the Lord your God, He is the One who goes with you. He will not leave you nor forsake you"* (Deuteronomy

31:6). He will provide comfort in sickness, debt, marriage problems, and addictions. Be of good courage. God is not going anywhere.

God wants you confident in this truth, that through Him all things are possible. Our confidence comes from our relationship with God, and it's through confidence and belief that our lives take on new stability, focus, and direction. We put no confidence in the flesh, but we have every confidence in the God who made us, called us, saved us, and keeps us.

I even tuned in to Benny Hinn's website as God used Him to lay hands on the sick (Mark 16:18). I could literally feel the anointing and the power of God through the monitor. God can do anything, take Him out of the box and watch Him work! Live a life of expectation and believe God for the greatest outcome. Be desperate and believe.

God does not seek to interfere with our happiness, but He does require that we relinquish our will. He cannot bless us as He desires to until our will is yielded up, and we accept His will in exchange. Jesus gave up His will in the garden of Gethsemane, "*Not my will but Thy will be done.*" God has a perfect will for your life. So many times we are in resistance to what God is doing. When we resist the process we're tampering with God's plan. We never know whose deliverance we are holding up, including our own. What if Jesus would have resisted God's will as He faced the cross? It's a scary thought to think about where we would be right now if Jesus had chosen His own will over God's will for Him. Mankind gained salvation because of Jesus' submission to God's will.

The Love of My Family

I had been praying for stronger family ties for years, especially
between my mother and I. Growing up as a teenager there were
times that I disrespected my mother by talking back to her. This
behavior caused a serious strain on our relationship the older I
became. God used this situation to draw my mother and me closer. I
called her and shared with her the things I found out during my
research on cancer. She would do her own research as well and was
very excited to share with me the information that she found. My
aunt believed I was healed when I didn't know that I was healed,
according to God's Word. She constantly spoke life and
encouragement to me. My sister called me every day to see how I
was feeling and exemplified so much compassion. My brother's
love and laughter always seemed to make things better. So much
good came out of my trials.

Back in Winston Salem

The time came again for me to be back in Winston Salem with my
husband on business. It was June by this time. I didn't dread being
there, but somehow it did strike up old memories simply because
that's where I discovered something was wrong. From January to
June everything had completely changed. I had no idea at the time I
found the knot in my thigh that so much would later transpire. A lot
of pain, frustration and healing had taken place within those six
months. I thought to myself, *"This is where it all began."*

While my husband was downstairs in the Regional Vice
Presidents meeting, I was in my hotel room praising and thanking

God. Even though I was going through what I was going through, God was bringing me through it, and I dared not complain. I had no other attitude except one of gratefulness.

Taking it Day by Day

From January until then, I had endured a lot, but at least I was still alive. I actually felt better than I had ever felt in my life. The diet change, along with exercising made a huge impact on the way I felt. Through exercising, I found a new way to relax and mentally distress.

I have had women and men ask me if I would help them with weight loss because I had lost so much weight. I proceeded to tell them that the first thing they should do would be to cut out all sugar and breads, and drink only water with plenty of exercise on a regularly basis. The exact words I get most of the time are, *"You mean to tell me no sweets?"* Once again, our desire gets us in trouble because not everything that tastes good is good for us. However, there are people who took my advice and began to lose their weight and feel healthier as I did.

I hear people say all the time there aren't enough hours in a day. Unfortunately, there are always going to be things that keep us distracted. This world is so demanding, and we are often pulled into so many directions. We must be willing to change. We can't change the direction we're going in until we change the way we think. This often calls for us to make conscious efforts to do better. Some things are more important than others. I would say that our health takes top priority, so we must exercise ourselves in the Lord first by reading and studying His Word on a daily basis. Second, exercise and take care of our physical bodies.

Cancer Statistics

I read in a 2014 annual report about cancer facts and Figures that there have been 1,665,540 new diagnoses this year alone, and over 585,720 deaths in the U.S. This disease isn't slowing down; in fact it's getting worse. They call cancer the unstoppable killer. Richard Nixon declared war on cancer in 1971 and the National Cancer Institute has invested over $90 billion into research and treatments. Yet a cure remains elusive. We must stop taking our health for granted and be mindful of what we are putting into our bodies. Get ahead of this disease now and protect the environment of your body through herbal teas and supplements, also coupled with a diet and lifestyle change. Life offers no guarantees. There will be more cancer statistics towards the end of this book.

Chapter Fourteen

The Lord Delivers

There's nothing that gets God's attention more than the suffering of one of His saints. *"Many are the afflictions of the righteous but the Lord delivers us out of them all"* (Psalms 34:19**)**. I have to say, there are some steps that you must take when believing God for your healing. First, you must confess any sins you may have, and turn from them. Have no unforgiveness or bitterness in your heart. If you expect to get God's attention you must come before Him with a pure heart. You must let God see that you want Him, and not just for what He can give, or do for you. I knew that if I expected Him to move on my behalf, I had to live according to His Word. I had to study His Word in order to know how to live by it. I didn't want anything standing in the way of my relationship with God.

God has a perfect will and plan for our lives, and at some point we all will face some form of suffering. When we suffer for righteousness sake, God is after something that only suffering can produce and bring forth. Suffering teaches us to have a submissive heart and makes us more determined to obey God's word. It purifies us through submission to God in prayer and regular study of His word. It produces more fruit, compassion, direction and patience. *"My brethren, count it all joy when you fall into various trials, knowing that the testing of your faith produces patience. But let patience have its perfect work that you may be perfect and complete, lacking nothing."* (James 1:2) This doesn't mean that we deny or ignore the pain of suffering and grief. It means that suffering and grief can lead to joy, for trouble provides an opportunity for us to deepen our relationship with Christ and to learn how to walk more intimately with Him. We also have the ability to become more holy when we encounter suffering.

Take Job for instance, the Bible says that he was a perfect and upright man, one who feared God and shunned evil. Job suffered for no wrongdoings of his own. God allowed Satan to have his way with Job to prove to the enemy that Job wasn't serving Him for material things. Job had his moments where he wondered what was going on. He doubted himself, but never God. When we are faced with different trials, we must display the patience and endurance that Job had. Every trial is not sent to destroy you; sometimes God uses your sufferings to develop you, and silence the devil.

Your troubles are not always about you. God is always up to something. Sometimes our troubles come because we live in a fallen world where disease spreads, babies get sick and innocent people die. Sometimes we suffer not because of doing wrong, but because of doing what's right.

"The Lord is not slack concerning His promise, as some count slackness, but is longsuffering toward us, not willing that any should perish, but that all should come to repentance" (2 Pet. 3:9). I love this scripture because it clearly shows His desire for us all to be saved. God, if He chooses could immediately destroy us in our sins. Because we were created for Him and by Him, every day that He allows us to wake up is another opportunity to repent and turn to Him. God is a perfect example of longsuffering, meaning He's slow

to anger and never gives up on us. He allows something's to happen to us for a greater purpose, and usually it's more than we can see or understand. There are times when God will take a life in order to save it from the path of hell. I know that may sound crazy but it's true and that's love, especially if one of His children is on a path of self-destruction.

The suffering I faced taught me to lean and depend on God. It's a bit sad to say, but true. If most people are not suffering with some sort of sickness, financial problem or some kind of heartache, we would rarely ever look to God. The fact of the matter is most people do not accept Christ into their lives until they are down and out and experiencing hardship. That's why you hear so many stories of men and women getting saved while they're in jail. There is nothing wrong with that; God knows what it is going to take to get our attention. We need suffering sometimes to keep us near, or bring us to the cross.

Mentally, cancer is by far the most difficult thing I have ever dealt with. For once, I was included in the statistics. I wondered how I had gotten to this place. I thought betrayal at its worse. To be betrayed is to compare something to an enemy. You may have friends and family turning on you, but you wouldn't think you would be betrayed by your own body. I wasn't eating properly, nor was I getting an adequate amount of exercise. I used to get colds and the flu fairly easily, as well as painful sore throats, but I never attributed those ailments to having a compromised immune system. Years later, when I was diagnosed I shouldn't have been caught off guard, but I was. My body had been trying to tell me all those years something was wrong. It was as if my body began to scream at me saying, *"Can you hear me now!"* I heard it loud and clear, and I definitely got the message. I was totally negligent when it came to the well-being of the temple that God had given me. Therefore, I had to deal with the consequences.

Who Are You Listening To

There are so many people who do not like themselves, and struggle with self-hatred, a lack of self-esteem and guilt. How can you not love yourself if God loves you? How can you not forgive yourself if God is willing to forgive you? We sometimes deny Gods statement of love and therefore are in direct opposition to God.

Instead of us listening to God tell us how beautiful and perfect we are in Him, we listen to the lies of the enemy telling us how sorry we are, and how we are not going to amount to anything. Listening to the lies of the enemy causes us to struggle with how we see ourselves.

The enemy tells you, that you're sick with cancer or some other disease, and automatically you believe the lie that says, this disease is incurable. You automatically believe that you're going to die, even if someone came along and offered you alternative treatments. This has happened to me on so many occasions. Whenever I encountered people that were faced with cancer; I would share my story with them and offer assistance in helping them get well through information. I was often told that the disease was incurable and it's too late. Let me ask you a question, do you think that God needs to use sickness to get you to heaven? The disease doesn't have to be incurable, stop believing the devils lies. Every sickness is not unto death.

Moses prophesied that your lifetime should be 70 to 80 years, anything less than that is not God's will. *"The days of our lives are 70 years; and if by reason of strength they are 80 years, yet their boast is only labor and sorrow; for it is soon cut off, and we fly away, who knows the power of Your anger? For as the fear of You, so is Your wrath. So teach us to number our days that we may gain a heart of wisdom"* (Psalms 90:10-12).

If you are less than 80, I would say that you have a lot more living to do. Get up and encourage yourself In the Lord, and watch Him back you up with His word. Whose report are you going to believe?

Chapter Fifteen

Life in the Vine

As you go through your trials, are you becoming more like Jesus, or are you looking like your situation? I was told quite often that I didn't look like I was sick, which I quickly rebuked. I don't use the word *"sick"* at all concerning myself. I said that to say, you don't have to look like what you've gone through. It should be our goal to take on the appearance and the example of Christ. Through every form of persecution or distress, Christ showed meekness and humility. Our desire is to be conformed to His image. We are to live as He lived, and draw souls to the Lord. The more you focus on God, the more your circumstances will begin to change. A transformation will begin to take place. His thoughts will become your thoughts. His purpose will become your purpose, and the manifestation of His promises will begin to unfold. The fruit showing that you belong to Christ will become evident.

This fruit that I'm talking about produces righteousness and holiness in God our Father that draws others to Him. We absolutely cannot bear fruit outside of God. *"Abide in Me, and I in you. As the branch cannot bear fruit of itself, unless it abides in the vine, neither can you, unless you abide in Me. I am the vine, you are the branches. He who abides in Me, and I in him, bears much fruit; for without Me you can do nothing"* (John 15:4-5).

To abide means to dwell and stay there. It symbolizes our relationship with the Father. As the Vine, Jesus is the source of life and the source of fruitfulness. The person who has a continual intimate fellowship with Jesus will produce much fruit. Apart from Him, you will not produce fruit it doesn't matter how hard or how much work you do on your own.

The Bible often uses the metaphor of fruit to describe the produce of our lives. *"Even so, every good tree bears good fruit, but a bad tree bears bad fruit. A good tree cannot bear bad fruit, nor can a bad tree bear good fruit"* (Matthew 7:17, 18). When we live our life in the flesh, desiring the unholy and unnatural things of the flesh, we bore the fruit of self-destruction which comes from sin leading to death and disease. *"The fruit of the righteous is a tree of life, and he who wins souls is wise"* (Proverbs 11:30). Fruit is a direct result of whatever controls our hearts.

As branches cling to the vine, we cling to Christ, drawing our very life from Him. Fruits begin in the heart with the fruit of the Spirit. This inner fruit affects outward actions; our words and activities will glorify the Lord and the will of the Father will be accomplished.

"For in Him we live, move and have our being" (Acts 17:28). There is never a time that I don't need God. He sustains me moment by moment, and I would have lost my mind if it wasn't for Him keeping me. Think about it for a moment; you will quickly realize He kept you too when you thought you weren't going to make it. You may have felt like giving up, but you are still here. It's all because of Him; in Him is our very existence. He is the air that we breathe. As long as you stay connected to the Vine, you can make it through anything.

This means that I am in Christ Jesus; my life is not my own. All things that I encounter in this life revolve around my relationship with the Lord.

For I Know the Plans

Can you have a relationship with your spouse, friend, or family member if you don't invest time in them? The answer is no. You must take time to get to know your loved ones, what their needs are, their likes, and dislikes. You can tell by the look on their faces, or the way they are acting if something is wrong. Most importantly, you know their hearts. If you don't know what it means to have a relationship, or how to cultivate one, then you won't know how to have one with Christ. We can't be fooled into thinking we can buy our way into ones heart or go long periods of time without communication, or have no trust and think we're in a thriving relationship. It's not so. Our relationship with God is more important than anything and anybody. As you spend time with Him in prayer, meditation, and the study of His word, you begin to learn His heart and see His ways. You understand that He has a bright future planned for you, even though you may experience darkness, His light is always shining. It's His plan to bring you out. Nothing can hold you back, not even sickness or hardship.

"For I know the thoughts that I think toward you, says the Lord, thoughts of peace and not of evil, to give you a future and a hope" (Jeremiah 29:11). Based upon this scripture I knew that I had a blessed future ahead of me. One filled with promises and hope. God may have allowed the cancer, but it truly was for a greater purpose

not designed to end my life. I understood this because of His Word. Satan doesn't care that you read your Bible as long as you don't understand it, or apply it to your life. He will continue to feed you lies if you don't know the word of God.

Cancer is not a death sentence. Change your perception and stop looking at it in this way. Whatever you think, tell yourself, or believe, is what will manifest. That eviction notice that you may have gotten doesn't mean you're going to be on the streets. Just because everyone else is getting laid off from their job, doesn't mean you're going to be next. Once again stop looking at it this way. Change your thoughts. Change your life. Hope in the Lord, trust His promises, and never lose confidence in His ability to save you.

God Use Me

Sharing my faith became my focus. It was no longer about my pain and suffering. God really began to send me forth to speak and encourage others. This was the ultimate act of faith, and of course, the ultimate reward. I couldn't look to my own natural abilities. I was empowered by the Spirit as I continued to walk in faith.

I remember going to the home of a woman who had breast cancer. Now, as I mentioned earlier, I believed if God sent me to a person, He wanted to heal them. I arrived at the home of Ms. Gladys. She was a beautiful lady who had cancer years earlier, but the cancer returned. God used me to minister to her and her family. Her husband was very quiet, yet attentive, I'm sure he was curious as to why I was there. Their daughter Sharon was a good friend of mine. She knew some of the things I had been through and thought I could share my faith and my experience to help her mother.

I could tell that her mother and father had never heard of anyone being healed from cancer without the standard treatments. I spoke with the family and shared my faith. I could see that Ms. Gladys began to be encouraged. She asked me, *"How did you get started on the natural path?"* By the time I was getting ready to answer her; a commercial came on the television. It was First Lady Reva McCluney and Pastor promoting a commercial for their church (New Harvest). I immediately lit up and said *"She's the lady who shared her faith with me when I didn't know what I was going to do. God used her, and I received direction!"* That was my first time seeing their commercial, and it confirmed in that moment that God was in the midst of everything I was doing.

I continued to talk with the family and tell them some things they could do. I shared with her different teas she could drink. Upon my leaving, I felt the need to lead the family in prayer. As the prayer was being prayed, the power of God filled the room. By the time I left, Mrs. Gladys husband had an entirely different demeanor, and I could see he'd been encouraged. He was smiling and feeling very hopeful, praise God! I love it when God uses little ole me to share and encourage one of His troubled saints.

Shortly after my meeting with Mrs. Gladys and her family, I received a call from my husband telling me a woman named Ms. Jackie had liver cancer. He wanted to know if I would be willing to speak with her. *"Of course"* I said, after all helping people was my new focus. I called Ms. Jackie, and we scheduled a time to meet. She was a very sweet spirited and quiet woman. She had been to several doctors who showed a lack of compassion during her visits. She was tired and needed help. Once again God used me. I began to explain to her about her diet and things she needed to stop eating, and shared some herbs that she should take. I immediately referred her to Terry the woman that I mentioned earlier that owns Creative Health. There, she received more guidance about reversing the cancer. Within months, without chemotherapy or radiation, Ms. Jackie was cancer free, praise God! She became serious about changing her eating habits, and was consistent with taking her herbs. She also used water, rest, and exercise as a part of her healing process.

Fruit of our Lips

"By Him therefore let us offer the sacrifice of praise to God continually that is the fruit of our lips giving thanks to His name" (Hebrews 13:15). I want you to try something for me. Stop whatever it is you're doing, and offer up to God the sacrifice of praise. You might as well. You want Him to show up in your situation don't you?

Don't praise Him because I'm asking you to; praise Him because you know He is worthy. Start singing songs of praise and thanksgiving. Whenever I have a lot on my mind, I get so full and lifted when I sing songs about the power of the blood. Usually these songs come from one of the old hymn books from back in the days. A lot of those old hymns have so much power and meaning behind them. At work, home, or in your car start singing.

Find a song that minister to you concerning your situation. You will be amazed at how you start to feel; you will soon forget about all of your problems. Time will pass and you will notice you haven't thought of that situation in hours. Stay connected to the Vine by keeping your heart right, and your spirit and faith lifted. Keep praying and stand strong. Keep singing and keep believing. Be encourage, you will make it through!

What Are You Teaching Your Children?

Growing up, my family was considered to be of the lower class. In spite of, my mother was a very strong woman; who did a great job at raising five kids on her own. I truly thank God for her. We didn't have a lot, but she instilled morals, values and the significance of faith, and a relationship with Christ in each of us. You may be reading this book, and money may not be an issue for you. Your family lives in a nice home, your children go to the best schools, and there seems to be no lack at the present moment.

Although everything seems good from a financial standpoint, ask yourself, *what am I instilling in my children?* Are they learning about the importance of being a child of God, and having faith in Him? Are you teaching your children about morals and values, or are you just providing them with things that money can buy and considering this doing your job as a parent? Providing financially is great don't get me wrong, but you're going to be held accountable for the things that you teach and don't teach your children such as reading God's word. My only purpose in bringing this up is due to the fact of how I was raised helped me with future problems. The things that were instilled in me taught me faith and how to overcome life's challenges. Money could not buy that.

My mother never let her children see her sweat. She never cried in front of us and never showed any weakness. I think back and today, I'm very grateful that God gave me the mother that He did. I truly would not be who I am today without her.

Let your children see Christ in you. Don't be one of those people that act so holy out in public, but at home you act as if you don't know who Christ is. You walk around being mean and nasty, always yelling, fussing and cursing. Your children will never look at you as the spiritual leader of your home with this type of behavior. Always exemplify Christ in everything you do. Your children's perception is being formed at a very early age. What they see you do, is usually what they will do.

Never give Up

On a particular cancer discussion board, a message came in from a guy whose dad was diagnosed with stage four pancreatic cancer. He was having a hard time dealing with it and believed his dad was dying. I could tell he turned to the discussion board for support and comfort. We all need comforting and encouragement at times. One ladies post stuck out to me. It read, "*Just make him comfortable and reminisce with him on all the good times you both shared. "Why would she write that?"* I asked myself. For some people, it seems easier to give up than it does to fight and have faith in God.

Her attitude was one of defeat. We all know cancer is a serious illness, but Jesus can turn anything around. I wrote to him; *"Take matters into your own hands; it's not over until God says so. You guys have to fight. Get on the Internet and begin to look up natural cures for pancreatic cancer. Search out scriptures, pray and trust God. Cancer can be reversed even in stage 4."*

Please guard your ear gate. Some people will think they are offering you good advice, but it could very well be the wrong advice. It also depends on the person who's ill. If they haven't mentally given up, and have enough strength to fight, then we should fight with them.

As I shared my story, one guy on the discussion board wrote to me and said that I would have to live with the disease and that cancer can't be reversed. He said cancer has to be maintained and that a person could live with it and treat it, but it would never go away. Well my thought was, *"the devil is a liar!"* There's no way in the world I would adopt that mindset. I'm telling you, the enemy will sneak in any way he can to knock you off your course. It doesn't matter what the situation maybe. Watch as well as pray.

It's during those times that you stand firm in your faith and tell the devil what the Lord said, just as Jesus did when the enemy was trying to tempt Him. When the enemy comes your way with all sorts of lies or accusations remind him just as Jesus did, *"It is written."* God's word is our most important weapon. Open up your mouth, and fight with the word of God as you declare your healing.

Too many times we are fighting with the wrong weapons. People are using guns, knives and weapons to harm one another. You think your spouse or your children are your enemy? Stop fighting with

110

physical weapons and fight with the Word of God. Understand who your opponent is, and stop taking your anger and frustrations out on those in your own household, or those that you love.

Stop letting him toy with your emotions. Stop believing his lies and stop letting him cause havoc in your life. It was a good thing I recognized the lies of the enemy. I would no doubt be worse off now than I had ever been if I didn't. The lie was, *"Chemo will make you better, and after that, the cancer will be all gone."* But we serve a God who is certain, and His promises always come to pass. "*For all the promises of God in Him are yes, and in Him Amen to the glory of God through us*" (2Corinthians 1:20).

Chapter Sixteen

Lies of the Enemy

When I was between the ages of eight and 10 years old, I can remember going into my mother's room around two or three in the morning, kneeling by her bed and repeating the words, *"I'm dying, I'm dying, I'm dying!"* I remember I hadn't been feeling well, and it felt like I was getting worse. At the time, I didn't realize it was the enemy because I was so young. However, as I got older and looked back over my life, I recognized a spirit of fear. It had paralyzed me at an early age. As a child, I couldn't go to the doctor except for yearly and routine checkups, if my mother considered something to be minor or if it wasn't serious, she wasn't taking us. My mother never entertained sickness, and neither did we. As I got older, I begin to notice different changes in my body; changes that caused me to fear and seek physicians for answers.

I remember once having a line going down the middle of my finger nail. I found myself at the doctor's office, because I thought something was seriously wrong only to learn it was completely normal. The doctor said it was some type of pigment in my skin. In another instance, there was a time where my eyes turned yellow around my pupils. I remember being really afraid as I went back to the doctor. Although I was diagnosed with an eye disease, it still wasn't serious. As long as I could see, I was fine. The doctor told me my eyes were very sensitive to the UV rays in the sun as well as the harsh winds. He said I would have to use a certain type of eye drop and wear sunglasses. Throughout my life there were numerous situations that truly weren't that serious, but caused me to seek out physicians. Later, I came to realize that this behavior was a phobia. A phobia is defined as a strong, persistent fear of situations, objects, activities, or persons.

It's so strange that even though sickness wasn't accepted in my household, the older I got, the more I began to entertain the enemy's lies concerning sickness. I had moments when I feared sickness and disease and I needed to get myself together, but when it came to cancer, I just couldn't accept it! I would not accept it!

Once I came to know Christ and began to grow in the knowledge of His word, I realized that phobias were not of God. We have no need to fear anything. *"For God has not given us a spirit of fear, but of power and of love and a sound mind"* (2Timothy1:7). As you begin to reclaim your mind and thoughts from the enemy, know that he won't easily give up the grip he has on your mind. Often we must stand against his lies and combat them with God's truth. I had to declare that I wouldn't allow any outside force to do my thinking; man or any spirit other than the Holy Spirit.

At Violas House

I talked earlier about how attitude determines outcome. Well, God led me to a woman whose name is Viola. It was through her that I learned I still had a long way to go. As I continued to lose weight, my dress size dropped drastically. I went from a size 12 to a size four in what seemed like overnight. This was very hard for me. My clothes would be so big on me that I didn't feel comfortable wearing them.

It was as if I was swallowed up by my own clothes. I was shopping all of the time because my weight was constantly dropping. I know women love to shop, but as the weight dropped, I had to shop for a different size each time. It soon became aggravating and expensive. Not to mention, I had bought summer dresses during the winter that I planned on wearing the next summer.

However, by the time summer came around my life had changed, as well as my size. I had a closet full of new clothes that I couldn't wear. I had to be a blessing to someone, so I gave them all away, except the size eight and a few of the size 10 dresses that I loved and decided to keep. I was determined that one day I would fit into them again. I trusted the Lord would provide for me as I blessed someone else. After a while, I started going to consignment shops to buy clothes. It became easier and less expensive. I would often find great deals and name brand clothes for a little of nothing and thus brought back my shopping excitement.

I called Viola, a good friend of mine who was a seamstress. When I got to Viola's house, I told her I had a few dresses that needed alterations. She could see that I had lost a lot of weight and thought I looked good. Every time she gave me a compliment about my size, I would put myself down. I thought I looked like a person who used drugs, because I was so small. My face was sunken in and you could literally see the bones in my cheeks. I felt so skinny, and that's how I thought people saw me. My husband kept telling me there were a lot of women who would love to be a size four.

Talking with Viola and thinking back on some of the things my husband had previously said, I realized how negative my behavior was, not concerning the illness, but concerning my appearance. So I began to pray and ask God to help me to see myself the way that He sees me, and to help me love myself the way He loves me. I finally realized it didn't matter how people viewed me, but how I viewed myself. I'm not saying it was easy. It really was a long process. To this day, it's a process that I'm still working on. I have to encourage myself every day and remind myself of how much God loves me.

I had to learn to love myself again. God's love is so strong, powerful, and transforming. If I could love myself with that type of love, then I would be okay. I'm not quite there yet, but I'm learning His love doesn't just apply to Him loving us, or us loving others, but it also applies to us loving ourselves. No matter what, know that you are special and God loves you. My physical appearance had changed because of losing the weight, but love should never be based on how you or someone looks. Love is so much deeper than that. If God loves me through my imperfections, flaws and shortcomings, then I could love myself, and you could love yourself too. *"There is no fear in love, but perfect love casts out fear, because fear involves torment. But he who fears has not been made perfect in love"* (1John 4:18). I realized I didn't understand God's perfect love. His love is a flow of compassion and sacrifice. We may not know how to give this type of love, but I suggest we love by faith, and ask God to perfect His love in us. God's love in us, loves for us. Love is so powerful, it changes things and circumstances.

Chapter Seventeen

When Things Seem Impossible

One day while watching the movie, *Facing the Giants;* I remember this particular scene in the movie where the coach blind- folded one of the players and made him carry this kid on his back 50 yards across the finish line. The guy carrying the kid on his back started out strong, but as time progressed, the weight of the football player on his back became heavier and heavier. The kid didn't think he could go on, but his coach kept telling him, *"Come on, you can do it. You're half way there, don't give up!"* The kid would yell, *"I can't, it's too heavy, I'm* tired!" but he kept going, giving it all he had. He was tired, sweating, his knees were buckling, but he kept going. The weight of the kid he was carrying on his back seemed to take all of his strength, but he never gave up. His coach continued yelling, *"You can do it, don't give up!"* Before he knew it, the guy removed his blind fold and noticed he had carried a 160 pound kid on his back across the entire football field. The weight will get heavy at times, and even though it seems that God is nowhere around, we must continue moving forward. The blind fold represented the fact that we walk by faith and not by sight. You may not see your way, or see how you're going to come out of that dark situation, but don't give up. You never know how strong you are until being strong is the only choice you have.

You will get to the end zone if you faint not. My faith was recharged. God gave me faith boosters along the way to keep me encouraged and lifted. I had a lot of moments where I was up and down in my emotions. One minute I exercised great faith, and the next minute I didn't know how I was going to make it through.

When I looked back over the months, I saw how the thing that seemed impossible was made possible by my faith in God. I was actually doing it. I remember in the beginning thinking, how in the world was I going to live and act as if cancer was not the diagnosis? How was I going to turn down all treatments? But as months went by the emotional and mental storms that I was facing were slowly passing.

I heard about a woman who had been battling cancer for 23 years. I thought about the pain and the weariness she must have been feeling. I had been dealing with it several months and that was trying enough. I heard about so many others who were battling cancer and was touched by their stories. I continued to pray for others, because I realized that prayer was the only way any of us could make it through.

I chose to look at the role of caregivers, understanding they are often afraid, exhausted, and worn down themselves. Whether caring for a chronically ill elderly person, a spouse, or parent this role can physically and mentally take a toll on anyone. It doesn't matter how strong you are.

For marriages, the vows say, *"in sickness, and in health,"* which was my situation. My husband stepped up with love and support. I saw another side to him that was pleasing. When you enter a marriage and recite your vows, at some point those vows will be tested. It made us take a look at our marriage and we realized the love we have for each other is greater than any situation that we could ever go through.

God's Word, Our Guide

God revealed to me that you must continue to confess the Word. Take your eyes off the situation, which I know is hard at times, and put them on God. Really believe the Word, and stop talking about how bad things are, or how bad you feel. Get your mind and your spirit right *"I will lift up mine eyes unto the hills, from whence cometh my help"* (Psalms.121:1). Please realize your help comes from the Lord. Like I said earlier, I sowed seeds toward my healing. I sent out prayer requests all over the world. I would visit different Internet sites watching Benny Hinn and countless other ministries that encouraged me. People I knew were interceding for me at church and in corporate prayer. I would call up prayer request lines and have people pray with me, as well as spend time in prayer at the park. I absolutely had no shame in asking others to pray for me.

I read about how the Lord delivered the three Hebrew boys from the fiery furnace because they wouldn't worship a golden idol like everyone else. They had so much confidence in the God they served. They were willing to accept punishment for not bowing down to the idol. God delivered them and honored their faithfulness. When we take a stand for God, whether it is for doing what's right, or just exercising our faith, God honors us and will deliver us. *"The righteous cry out, and the Lord hears, and delivers them out of all their troubles"* (Psalms 34:17).

For the Glory of God

There was a man in the bible which was born blind from birth. The disciples asked Jesus, *"Master, who did sin, this man, or his parents, that he was born blind?"* Jesus answered, *"Neither hath this man sinned, nor his parents; but for the works of God should be made manifest in him"* (John 9:1-3). The healing of the blinded eyes was for the glory of God. There are still situations like this today. Sickness doesn't always mean sin is involved. However, I do think it is a good idea to examine your life, your relationship with God and others when dealing with sickness. Self-examination is always a good thing. You never know what could be hindering your healing from coming forth.

Nevertheless in the blind man's case, God used his disability to show His great power and to exude His absolute mercy. Who knows why God does what He does, and who can challenge, or question Him. His ways are absolutely perfect. He has a reason and a plan for everything He does. He is God!

Absentee Dad

After I was diagnosed with Hodgkin's Lymphoma, I began the self-examination process. I had to deal with potential spiritual road blocks that could hinder God from healing my body. The more I researched Hodgkin's, the more I realized this disease originated from deep rooted bitterness, or abandonment associated with unresolved rejection by a father.

I grew up without a father. The closest persons I've ever had as male role models growing up were my three brothers; especially my younger brother Jeffrey. He has always been a good man. He treats his daughters and wife like queens, just as a father would his daughter. As we were growing up, he always looked after my sister and I, making sure we had whatever we wanted. He was always kind and showed so much love towards us. To this day, we have a very close relationship; even though my whole family is close knitted. However, the rejection and the ache of not having a father left me empty. I never experienced the love a father has for his little girl, and therefore the ache began to grow in silence, to the point it could have been associated with this type of cancer.

I prayed that God would heal me from the mental damage of my past, the bitterness and all the ugly emotional pain that followed. I had to forgive my father, for not being there, even though I still have never seen him. I had to release that rejection and accept God's love and move forward. I couldn't dwell in that pain if I wanted God to heal me.

That Sneaky Devil

One day in particular, I was at the office and a business partner of ours came by and handed me a book about a woman who battled cancer. I was at first hesitant to read the book, but after a couple of days I picked it up and started to look it over. As I read, to my surprise, this woman had the same form of cancer I was diagnosed with. We both found the lymph node in our right thigh. She had all the beliefs that I had. She did the raw foods, the diet, the exercise, and the natural supplements just as I did. She was even out of town when she discovered something was wrong, just as I was.

Only one thing was different, and that was the way God healed us. I believed God had healed me by the power of His Word, and my faith was strong enough that I didn't have to take chemo and radiation. Remember, we did everything the same, but she strongly advised following the treatment plan the doctor ordered which was chemo and radiation. She said, *"I know you have to put all your faith in God and He is your healer, but you have to trust God to work through the doctors."* She said, *"I should take the medicine prescribed for me lest I become worse."*

Honestly, it was as if God Himself was speaking to me through her book, and I began to doubt everything I believed concerning my healing. Once again, fear stepped in, and I spent most of that day scared and confused. By the time evening had come, I had gotten myself together. I realized God wasn't the author of confusion and knew it had to be the enemy. I rebuked him on every hand and continued to believe God just as I had been doing. Then next day I received a call from my sister asking me if I was all right. She told me that God had awakened her around 4:00 that morning and had her praying for me. She asked me how I was doing with great concern in her voice.

I really couldn't talk because I was in front of some business partners at that time, so I told her I would call her back. When I called her back, I told her yesterday was a rough day for me. I told her everything I believed God was doing. I felt He was sending me in another direction. I believed that's why God had her praying for me. I was so grateful because God loved me so much that He woke someone up on my behalf to intercede for me.

I thought if God didn't care, He wouldn't have placed me on her heart. He would have just let me be. I thanked my sister for being obedient to His voice. God continued to show me how much He loved me, and that He was doing a great work in me for His glory. God loves us too much to leave us just as He found us. He knows our exact weaknesses and struggles. He knows we can't fight this battle alone and has people assisting us in the battle through prayer. Has God ever laid someone on your heart? If so, please don't ignore it, start praying. Because I guarantee you, God has people praying for you. You never know, what forces you may be combatting in the realm of the spirit. Your prayers could actually be saving someone's life during that very moment.

He has also assigned those who will assist you along the way. God has people who will be there to give you a word of encouragement just when you need it the most. He has that person who calls or drops by right on time asking, *"Do you need anything?"*

I thank God for my friend Roxanne, even though things got rough at times, we still found multiple reasons to laugh and just be silly. Talking with her made my heart glad. It allowed me, for a moment, to forget everything I was currently dealing with. I love this woman, and to this day I can't remember half the things we laughed about. She was just as important to me as someone asking me if I needed anything.

My husband made sure I was always okay. If he was at work and I was having a bad day, he would immediately come home and sit with me. He made sure I had the emotional support I needed to get through this trial. God also placed a woman in my life by the name of Bonita. She works in the business with us. She has a quiet spirit and is a beautiful strong woman of God. Her personality was different from mine, but we had one thing in common, *Jesus.* We were able to connect in the spirit as she stood in faith with me believing God had already healed me. Whenever I had a doctor's appointment, I would call her, and she would pray with me for a favorable outcome.

Even though I had gotten myself together and my faith was back on track, I told Bonita about the book I had read and what it did to me. She began to speak words of life to me and basically told me every situation was different. I had to continue to trust and believe God just as I had always done, and not lean to my own understanding. Her words were powerful and bore witness with my spirit. I was able to receive everything she said. She is just one of the many beautiful women God placed before me, and our relationship grew from there.

Back at Dr. Yee

The time had come for another doctor's visit. I had been waiting for Emory to call back and schedule me for a new PET and CT scan. A lot of changes had taken place and I felt I was definitely on the right track. We had been waiting a little over a week for Emory to call back, but they never called. I assumed maybe God closed that door because He was going to open up another door. My husband wasn't as impatient as I was and thought we should continue to wait for them to call.

The time had come for me to return to Gibbs Cancer Center to have my blood drawn. When I walked in all the staff thought I looked really good. They were giving me compliments that made me feel great especially since I had been struggling with my self-image. Little did I know they were thinking I looked good for a person taking chemo. Once I was in the office, they immediately called me back to have my blood drawn. All of a sudden, a nurse who I had never seen before came out. I could see she was in a rush as she prepared to draw my blood.

She wasn't the normal person who usually drew my blood. Her first words were, *"I came to draw blood from your port."* I was thinking to myself, *"Huh?!"* My husband caught on faster than I did and immediately said, *"She doesn't have a port because she didn't take chemo."* The nurse had a look of confusion on her face and said, *"You are Reschelle Means, aren't you?"* I told her, *"yes,* but *I didn't take chemo."* She gave my husband and I a strange look as if she was thinking, *"I wish someone would have told me before I got here."*

She was sent there specifically to draw my blood. As we were talking my phone started vibrating; to my surprise it was Emory University finally calling back to schedule an appointment. I thought that was odd, because I had been waiting over a week for them to call, and I was in the middle of an appointment. I didn't understand what was going on, but I knew God was in the midst. While my husband was on the phone with Emory, I proceeded to get my blood drawn from my arm as I had previously done. The doctor asked me all sorts of questions, such as *"have you been feeling well? Are you having night sweats? Do you have any sores in your mouth? Have your ears been hurting?"* I answered, *"No"* to all of his questions. When I was first diagnosed, I had night sweats, and my ears ached from time to time, but that's not the reason I went to the doctor. Once I knew what I was dealing with and started praying and treating myself, I never had any more of the symptoms the nurse asked me about.

"The spirit of a man will sustain him in sickness, but who can bear a broken spirit? (Proverbs 18:14) The spirit and the mind govern the body, but not that of the body to govern the mind. Therefore, when the body is under attack, the spirit sustains him. This spirit the Bible speaks about is one that has been renewed by the power of God and washed in the precious blood of Jesus.

Letters from My Class

When I found the knot and was told it was cancer, I had to withdraw from school. Mrs. Robinson, my public speaking teacher had the whole class to send me cards of encouragement through the mail. The cards had the following comments; *"Reschelle, you are a strong woman of God, and He will bring you through this. Hold on to your faith, and never doubt God."* My eyes would tear up every time I read one of those cards. Once again, God was showing me how much He loved me as He encouraged me though their cards. The cards were totally unexpected and so much appreciated. I kept those cards in my purse. During my doctor's visit and times when my mind would begin to wonder, I would pull out those cards and read them. They gave me strength and encouragement. I realized others looked at me as being strong, even though that wasn't what I was trying to be. My strength truly came from the Lord. I read a quote that says, *"Failure will never overtake me if my determination to succeed is strong enough."*

Chapter Eighteen

The Gamble of the Treatments

Chemotherapy is a huge gamble. There are no guarantees it will get the cancer, or even if the cancer will not return. Since the outcomes of the treatments were not only damaging to my body, but also uncertain, I couldn't take that chance. The oncologist offers you treatments that are supposed to make you better, but most of the time you end up a lot worse off. I know a woman who took chemo and since then has had to go to dialysis three times a week, because of kidney failure. Another lady, Ms. Beverly who is very dear to my heart suffers from congestive heart failure as a result of the chemo. I also know of a woman who has developed Crohn's disease because of the treatments, and another man who says his body has never functioned properly since chemo.

Understand this Scenario

Imagine you have a dream home that you've lived in for years. It's beautiful and well maintained. It has all the amenities except it has termites inside. When you call the exterminators, they tell you they won't be able to target just the termites, as these termites are of an especially crafty breed. They tell you they're going to set off a series of explosions in your home that **may** kill the termites. They warn you, *"oh yeah, it may destroy some of your house in the process, some of your sheet rock will be destroyed in the process, the roof could possibly cave in, and the exterior may suffer great damages as well"* and their question to you is, *"hey, you wanted the problem fixed, didn't you?"* There's no way that you would allow them to

experiment with something that **may** get the termites, but offers **no** guarantees. You would try another method that doesn't involve the destruction of your home and has a greater chance of fixing the problem.

In this example at least the exterminator told you what may happen while getting the termites. With chemotherapy only a few side effects are ever mentioned. Your body is your temple (the home where the Spirit of the Lord dwells) and chemotherapy will destroy your body, just as the exterminator destroyed the home. If patients really knew the complete run down on the treatments and all the damage that it causes, I'm pretty sure that most of them would not take the treatments. I will take it one step further, if cancer patients knew there were alternative medicines they could take without the harmful side effects, and far less expensive I believe more people would take that route, just as I did.

Chemotherapy targets cells that are actively growing and spreading. Since conventional medicine does not offer much hope for incurable diseases, it's time we take back our power over disease, chart our own course, and take responsibility for our own destiny. Where there is life, there is hope, and even if one has already started taking the treatments, there are natural supplements that can still be taken along with the conventional medicine to limit the side effects. However, once a person has already taken chemotherapy and has been exposed to the toxic chemicals in their body, it lowers their chances of reversing the cancer even if alternative medicines are used, but God can turn anything around.

Based on my extensive research, the pharmaceutical industry as a whole is a $200 billion a year business and 97% of conventional cancer treatments not only fail miserably, but are almost guaranteed to make the patients sicker.

I read a statistic online that says,

- In the early 1900s, one in 20 people developed cancer
- In the 1940s, one in 16 people developed cancer
- In the 1970s, one in 10 people
- Today it is one in three people
- Two out of three people will die from the cancer they have been diagnosed with within five years.

My Daily Regimen

I put myself on a strenuous regimen that kept me extremely busy. There were a lot of days that I was completely overwhelmed. I was taking my supplements as scheduled, exercising, drinking this mix and that one, and doing everything I could to get healthy. Late one evening, I had just finished washing my hair and turned on the TV. For the first time, I heard Pastor Joseph Prince speak. His whole message was about grace, and the Word of God began to speak through him. I was already tired of the regimen, but I was willing to do what was necessary to be healthy.

My regimen included:

- Rebounding (jumping on a mini trampoline) 450 jumps in the morning and 150 at night

- I took nine natural supplements starting at 8:30 that morning. These supplements consisted of; selenium, garlic pills, Japanese Mushroom Vitamins, IP6 with Insole and Vitamin B17. I also drank Essiac Tea often throughout the day.
- I would make a homemade fruit juice that included: apples, pineapples, grapes, strawberries, pears, and blueberries at 8:45a.m.
- Six more supplements at noon, and for lunch I would eat beans and wild rice, or I would have a salad and some almond nuts
- 2:00 p.m. a sweet potato
- 3:00 that afternoon I took more natural supplements and drank a vegetable juice that consisted of leafy green vegetables
- 5:00 p.m. maybe a piece of grilled or baked chicken and a salad with organic salad dressing or beans
- Nine more supplements, 150 rebounds at 8:00 p.m., and another vegetable juice. I also put two tea-spoons of raw apple cider in my water every couple of days. I drank blueberry tea, a detox tea that cleans your liver and your colon. I began to take wheat grass powder once a day, no specific time. I drank Aloe Vera juice, and plenty of bottled purified and distilled water. I also started to take Raw Life, a green powder that has raw dried vegetables in the form of a green powder. I took this several times a day. Since there was a

problem with my lymphatic system, I used
Lymphatic drops several times a day in my water
that promotes healthy lymphatic function
- Between 9:30-10p.m. bedtime

The next day I did the same regimen all over again. This soon
became a continuing headache that was hard to continue. My
husband was spending a lot of money on supplements. I was
going to the grocery store about three times a week to buy fruits
and vegetables. I had to buy small amounts of fruits and
vegetables because they went bad easily. It cost between
$700-$900 a month to maintain and stay healthy. I'm not
complaining because I was willing to do whatever it took. In my
mind, the route I took was cheaper and less painful than the
treatments the doctors ordered. I was so grateful we had the
money to buy the things that I needed.

As I was watching television that evening, Pastor Prince so
profoundly spoke words that set me free from the headache of the
regimen. He said we are not under the law anymore, we are under
grace. The law says, *do, do, do* and grace say, *it's already been
supplied.* What I got from that message was; I had gotten so
immersed in everything I had to do to reverse the cancer that I began
to crucify Christ on the cross all over again. I had been set free from
the law, but didn't really understand it until God used Pastor Prince
to minister to me in that moment. I still took my pills and did my
juicing just as I had always done, but if for some reason I wasn't
able to take them, I chose not to fret over it. I had to ask myself, *"Do*

I really trust in God to heal me, or am I relying on these supplements?" This question got me to thinking. At that point I began to examine myself to see exactly where my faith stood.

This allowed me to know God on a completely different level. My faith was challenged and I had no choice but to grow and believe God if I was going to overcome cancer. Frances J. Roberts in his One Minute Meditation wrote: *"So long as there is disease in your thoughts, there will be disease in your body. Only when your mind is at rest can your body build health."* When your mind is at rest, you can have total peace. You experience peace when you put complete trust in God. *"Peace I leave you, My peace I give to you; not as the world gives do I give to you, Let not your heart be troubled, neither let it be afraid (* John 14:27).

Chapter Nineteen

A Prophetic Glimpse

It had been three months since I had my last PET and CT scan. I had eased up on the regimen, and it felt really good to be free from the schedule I had been restricted to. I spent every day in prayer while believing God had healed me. Finally, the moment I had been waiting for was near. By this time it was June, and I was anticipating going back to Emory getting my final scans out of the way, and returning in a week for the results.

I imagined the doctor telling me the cancer was gone. I heard about different people God healed; people who the doctors previously said had a certain disease, but later the disease was miraculously gone. People the doctors had given up on, but God healed them. I wanted to experience that same moment. I knew that if God could do it for those people, He could do the miraculous for me too. God had already given me a glimpse of all being well, so to actually hear the doctor say the cancer was gone would be the moment of victory. Actually, the victory was the glimpse, but I just needed to hear the words. God is so awesome. He will show you a glimpse of your outcome. He gives us prophetic glimpses to keep us believing and encouraged. If it wasn't for what He showed me my struggle could have been a lot worse.

A Visit with Terry

My doctor's appointment was on a Wednesday, and I had an appointment to see Terry on that Monday. When I arrived at

Terry's, she began to ask me all sorts of questions. I told her all of the things I was doing and the supplements I had been taking. She was very impressed and thought I had been doing a great job. I told her about the appointment I had on Wednesday to have my scans re-done. She was excited for me and believed with me that everything would be okay. Terry had Melanoma cancer about 20 years earlier, and was cancer free. She took no chemo or radiation. She explained how she had just come from Duke University having her scans done over and was grateful all her tests looked good.

In a couple of days it would be my turn and I was more than ready for that day to come. I wasn't quite as nervous this time as I was the first time. I had confidence in everything I had done to get me to that point. More importantly, I had complete confidence in God. My visit with Terry before the appointment gave me so much encouragement. Just to hear her say that she was proud of me made me smile, after all she was my mentor. Her test results were all negative and I believed God that all mine would be negative as well.

Toxins and Detox

Terry has always talked to me about toxins, so I wish to share with you concerning toxins that maybe in your body. It's a very good idea to make sure that the state of your body's environment is healthy, and conducive to your body operating to its healthiest full potential. Here let's deal with toxins, because toxins turn into disease.

Toxins are a chemical, or poison that is known to have harmful effects on the body. They can come from food or water, also from chemicals used to clean the house and even from the air that we breathe. Our bodies process these toxins through organs such as; the liver and kidneys, and eliminate them in the form of sweat, urine and feces. I heard a quote that says, *"You're not sick because you have cancer, you have cancer because you're sick"* When the body overdoses on toxins, disease forms in the body. Although the body is designed to heal itself, detox is how we must deal with the removal of toxins in the body.

Our bodies are smart; they have built in mechanisms to detox toxins. Our body's digestive, lymphatic and circulatory systems all play a major role in the process of detox. Look at it this way, just as you would spring clean your home making ready for the new season, detoxing your body should be looked at as a spring cleansing. It could be a fall, winter or summer cleansing, it really doesn't matter. I would definitely suggest after the holidays to do a serious detoxing. My husband and I have started doing a gall bladder cleanse. We found the recipe online. We both were amazed at the results. This cleanse also consisted of removing toxins from the liver and kidney. We were able to rid our bodies of backed up waste and to restore the environment of our body to its original healthy state of being.

This is one of the main ways to recharge, rejuvenate, and renew. Everyone can benefit from a cleansing. The only difference is there's no mop, vacuum, or dust rag needed for this cleaning. However, you will need to set aside some time which you can devote to the wellbeing of your health because toxins that are lodged in your cells, soft tissues, and muscles can overwhelm your entire immune system.

Here are some ways you can rid your body of toxins;

- Drink plenty of water; this helps you eliminate toxins through sweat, tears and urine.
- Practice deep slow breathing exercising, exhaling in and out, meditation is a good idea.
- Eliminate sugar and artificial sweeteners.
- Eat organic meets such as poultry fish and chicken.
- Develop a taste for fruits and vegetables and include them in your daily meals.
- Learn effective ways to deal with stress.
- Get plenty of rest.
- Get plenty of exercise and sunshine.
- Laugh more often.

For Your Information

Each day, we take in about 20,000 breaths and about 30 pounds of air. A single sneeze can send more than 5,000 respiratory droplets into the air at a speed of 47 mph. We are taking in so much from the environment we live in. I was watching the news one evening and the story was about a plant that had closed down. People that worked at that plant 15 years earlier were all being affected by the chemicals from the plant as well as those that had lived in the neighborhood for years. Needless to say, the toxins in the air exposed residents and employees to cancer, and a major lawsuit was underway. In some cases both spouses were affected.

Chapter Twenty

Victory at Last

Finally, the day had come for me to be back at the hospital to have all the scans done. I woke up that morning anxious and ready to get those tests done and over with. I thought about everything I had gone through that led me up to that point. My husband and I had to be at the hospital by 8:30a.m. I remember thinking to myself on the way; *"Lord, it's almost over, and soon Lord, You will avenge and deliver me."* We arrived on time, and after I finished filling out my paper work, I was called to the back immediately.

Once again, I was put into a small room as the nurse inserted the same substance into my body. I drank the same liquid every 30 minutes, while the nurse suggested I wrap myself up in a white blanket to preserve my body heat. This time my husband was allowed to come, and I felt a sense of peace with him in the room with me. I knew he had my best interest at heart. We talked, laughed and he encouraged me that this process was almost over. Finally, the hour was up and I was directed into the other room to have the scans done. At that point I was on my own. The scans lasted about 45 minutes. Everything went well and I was very glad that part was over with. The guy who did the scans had a great sense of humor which made the process that much smoother. After the scans were complete, I would have to wait until the following Wednesday for my results.

That would be my moment; the moment when everything that was wrong in my life would be right again. I wondered how the doctor

137

would tell me, and how he would be able to explain the cancer was gone without the normal treatments. I had all kinds of thoughts going through my mind.

In my waiting

I had finally finished my entire series of test, and all I had to do was wait for the final results. I would continue my daily study in God's word as I drowned myself in anything that was inspirational. I was doing my best to stay encouraged and found comfort in my family and friends. I continued to receive phone calls from people who knew about the cancer.

The more people called me, the more the enemy tried to tell me, *"You know they are only calling you because they think you are dying."* At first, I gave in to the lies of the enemy, not even realizing it. I would get a little upset with people when they called, because I was starting to believe they really thought I was dying. I had to put the devil in his place once I realized what he was doing. People who I hadn't heard from in years were calling me asking if everything was alright, and some even asked to take me to lunch.

God revealed to me that I had been there for so many people and sowed so many seeds of encouragement that I was just reaping what I had sown. God was using others to call and encourage me as I had done so often for others. Thank you to all who called, and encouraged me during that time.

Once again, as I waited to return to Emory the feelings of anxiety tried to overtake me. All I could do was continue thanking

God and was eagerly waiting to share what He had done. I know this seems crazy because I had already taken my last scans, but God was still dealing with me, even up until the last hour. While I was at church one Sunday, I became very distracted. As the Pastor was preaching, I could see his mouth moving, but I couldn't hear anything he was saying. As I sat there, I heard the Holy Spirit tell me, *"Repeat over and over, By His stripes you are healed."* Truly, my heart rejoiced when I heard those words. After all, this was one of my favorite Scriptures and one that I was very familiar with. I had already been listening to a CD from Oral Robert's ministry with so many scriptures on it. I have to say, it was refreshing to be able to quote just one and say it over and over until I felt the power of God moving in me.

I heard Dr. Creflo Dollar speak about how it didn't take a lot of scriptures. He said to find just one and use it as your weapon. I quoted and confessed, *"By His stripes I am healed."* I said that over and over with complete assurance that God had already healed my body, and I was just waiting on the manifestation of it through the doctor's report. I woke up one Monday, and I heard God say, *"Don't turn the TV on, and don't take any more supplements."* By this time I had already cut back and wasn't taking many. I paused for a second. It was not a problem with the TV since I had gotten use to not having it on anyway.

With the supplements, I wanted to make sure that it was God speaking to me and not the enemy or my own thoughts. I prayed and asked God, *"If this is You speaking Lord, show me."* When I opened my Bible, I came across the Scripture that read, *"Not by might nor by power but by my spirit says the Lord"* (Zechariah 4:6). I said, *"Okay God I hear You."* So for the next several days, I did just that. I took no supplements and chose to trust God. As I continued to believe God and thank Him for my healing, the illusions started again. It seemed like everything in my body began to ache.

My back began to hurt and I felt pains in my arms and stomach. There was a sore on the inside of my mouth, and my ears were even hurting. I also started having night sweats; all signs of cancer. I chose not to focus on the pain because I knew it was just an illusion and the enemy was doing anything he could to get me back on those pills and to doubt God. I had gotten to the point where I thought about everything that God was going to do, and all that He had already done. The devil couldn't touch me at that point.

Some Sweet Spirited Women

One day I was out shopping at one of the Boutique's in Greenville; the woman who worked behind the counter was shocked to see how much weight I'd lost. I was a regular customer and we frequently held conversation from time to time. As we talked, she began to ask questions about my weight. I explained to her I had been dealing with some health issues and had to change my eating habits. I explained to her about the raw food diet I had been on, which consisted of juicing vegetables. She couldn't understand why anyone would want to put themselves on such a rigorous diet and asked me, *"What was wrong?"*

I told her about the diagnosis and how I decided against chemo and radiation. I began to share my faith and that I was putting my trust in God. Before I knew it, people were standing around to hear my story. The people were intrigued and couldn't understand how in the world someone could be diagnosed with such an illness and refuse the treatments. I praise God for the opportunity to share my faith. I saw Anita there, a woman who I had met a couple years back. She and I began to talk about what had been going on with each other.

She was moved by what I had been going through and introduced me to Pam, a friend of hers who was also in the store. These two women had the love of God in them. They were thanking God because they had just told God they wanted to be more of a servant and help more people. Be careful what you ask for, because lo and behold they asked for someone, and God sent them me. They were so caring and so warm. I told them I had to be back at the doctor's office Wednesday for my results. They immediately called women together for prayer the next day. I received a text later that day with the address where we would be meeting. When I arrived, there were more women than I expected. I started thinking to myself, *"Did they call all these women here just because of me?"* However, it turned out that they were already meeting for an outreach gathering. During the meeting, we all held hands in prayer, believing God for favorable results for my upcoming appointment.

The power of God was so real in that place. Women and children were being healed and set free that evening. I was able to take my mind off myself, and see what God was doing in other people's lives. There was a teenage girl there who suffered from migraines. I praise God for the faith to lay hands on her and believe God for her healing. Once again, God showed me His love through those ladies. I was introduced to some beautiful women that night, and that was an experience I will never forget.

Finally, the Results

Finally, the day had come. My husband and I had to be back in Atlanta by 10:30 a.m. for the results of the scans I'd had done. I woke up very anxious that morning as I anticipated the results. My husband and I had a nice drive there as we reminisced over all that we had been through. When we arrived, we waited in the waiting area for almost an hour. As I sat there, my heart was so heavy. The room was full of patients that were suffering from cancer. As the nurse began to call our name, one by one, to go and have our blood drawn, more and more people continued to fill the room.

I saw women and men walking around with no hair. One lady was so weak, I'm assuming from the chemo, all she could do was lay on the sofa while her daughter kneeled down beside her on the floor as they waited for their name to be called. Some of the people there looked like I did. There were young, old and all different races in one huge waiting area. Cancer isn't prejudice. It doesn't target any specific person. Anyone, at any time, especially those with a history of unforgiveness, bitterness, rejection, poor eating habits, and those who smoke, may be subject to this disease.

As I sat there, I began to tell God how much I appreciated Him for not allowing me to suffer in the way that some of the others were sufferings. After all, I hadn't done anything so great. There are so many to this day who have lost their lives to this awful disease. I'm no different than any of them. I'm sure God loved them just as He loves me. Who knows what the future holds for any of us? My advice is to always stay connected to the Vine (Christ). Seek Him for who He is, not just for what He can do for you. I believe that God sovereignly controls every circumstance. As God guided me through this process, I realized He will not contradict His ways or His word. If He said it, then it shall come to past.

Please understand your need for Him, and to realize there's not ever one moment that you don't need Him. None of us deserved to be in this position. We all had different stories, different types of cancer, and we were all dealing with it in our own way. Sitting there, I could see the look on some of the loved one's faces. Some had the look of exhaustion, while I noticed one lady who couldn't stop biting her nails. What a stressful time it could be for anyone dealing with a situation of this nature. Please always pray for others. We need and rely on each other's prayers.

I was finally called back and put in a room where my husband and I waited for the doctor to come in. My moment had finally arrived. I longed to hear the words, *"The cancer is gone."* I had visions of celebrating and calling all my friends and family. I felt so many different emotions, one of which was fear. My husband seemed to be as cool as a cucumber, at least that's how he looked to me. I'm sure he was just as nervous as I was. I had a scripture in my purse. I pulled it out and began to read it silently, *"Fear not for I am with you; be not dismayed, for I am your God. I will strengthen you, yes; I will uphold you with My righteous right hand"* (Isaiah 41:10). The more I read this Scripture, more peace came over me.

The doctor finally came in with a 17 year old intern student. I was trying to read his facial expression. If he came in smiling, everything must be okay. If he had a look of dread on his face that meant something was wrong. Dr. Flowers looked at me with the most pleasant smile on his face and said, *"Mrs. Mean, your scans look fine, we don't see anything abnormal".* I sat there trying to get some understanding of what he was saying. It was as if he was beating around the bush with my results. My husband began to ask him questions because he wasn't talking fast enough for us. He spoke calmly as he tried his best to explain how the cancer had disappeared. It was obvious he had no idea.

He said, *"Everything looks good, but we need to redo the scans on your right leg, because the scans stopped at your upper thigh and we need to get more of your lower leg on the scans."* He said, *"Other than that everything looks okay."* Okay were not the words I was waiting to hear. I asked him, *"Are you telling me there is no cancer in my body?"* He said, *"Yes, there's no cancer showing up on your scans, and everything looks clear."* I asked him, *"What about my brain, are there any signs of cancer on my brain?"* He said, *"no, not a trace."* By this time I was screaming, *"Yes, yes, thank you Jesus, thank you Jesus!"* I was overjoyed and full of gratitude. My husband and I shared the biggest hug we had ever shared. God had proven Himself once again, and we both were in awe of His power. I was so grateful because what God did for some of the people I knew of, He did for me. Everything I went through wasn't in vain.

I couldn't think by this time, but the doctor was still talking. I told him he had to talk with my husband, because I was overflowing with emotions. When I calmed down, I looked at the doctor, pointed my finger toward him, and said; *"You know God did this right, God did this!"* All he could do was smile. The doctor probably thought I was crazy, but I needed him to know it was the power of God that healed me. The doctor wanted to talk more about having another scan done on my leg. As he was talking, I started praying silently. The doctor said to my husband and I, *"Excuse me for a minute,"* and left the room.

He came back within five minutes and said, *"There's no need to do additional scans. We got enough of your lower leg on the scans."* However, he told me I had to be back in three months for a follow up. If this is what the doctor ordered, I didn't mind, but I chose to live by faith and the power of God that the cancer would not return! I won't live in fear the cancer would come back like the enemy wants me to. I will continue to eat right and take care of myself. Now that I am more educated about this Intruder called cancer, I am able to share it with others.

Hearing the doctor say the cancer was gone was sweet melody to my ears. I looked over at my husband, who had the most beautiful and radiant smile on his face. It's one I will never forget. It was over for him as well. He showed so much compassion and was attentive during that time. We grew closer in our relationship. Our faith was challenged, but ultimately we rose to a new level in God. As we left the hospital, I heard a song in my spirit that's says, *"In the name of Jesus, in the name of Jesus, we have the victory, in the name of Jesus, in the name of Jesus, Satan, you have to flee!"*

I sung that song for days, even as I was sharing with people what God had done. Victory once again, was won that day and I was ready to spread the word to all who would listen; my God is a healer! That was truly a day of triumph for my husband and I, as well as our family and friends. God showed Himself and all were able to see and know that He is God. Before we left the doctor's office, my husband had already sent out a mass text telling everyone the news. I couldn't pick up a signal inside the hospital, but when I got outside, I called everyone in my contact list. I had people screaming, crying and thanking God with me the cancer was gone. God showed up in power and in demonstration; So that all could see and know He is Jehovah Rapha, the Lord who heals. There's nothing too hard for Him.

He is looking to show His power in the earth, and more importantly, He's looking for someone who will believe and know that He is able. As I told my friends, they told their friends. One lady wrote me and told me she had given her heart back to the Lord because of my story. That was confirmation what I went through was not in vain. I was walking into KFC to use the restroom and there appeared to be a homeless man sitting on the curb. I was so excited I said to him, *"The doctor just told me all the cancer is gone!"* I will never forget his words, *"It sounds like the Lord's doing to me."* I said, *"That's right Sir, God did it, and if you believe, there isn't anything He can't do for you!"* I was willing to share with anyone who would listen and tell them of the Lords mighty works.

Know that He is God

That evening Kerri and Quilla, a couple of girlfriends of mine joined me for a celebration dinner. Kerri was celebrating her divorce and Quilla was just grateful to be a part of the celebration. We all laughed, talked and had a great time. June 30, 2010 is a day that I will never forget. What God did in my life was bigger than me. God is saying, *"Be still, and know that I am God"* (Psalms 46:10). If you're sick, first know it's not God's will for you to be sick. Jesus came to destroy the works of the devil. He has come to give you life more abundantly, as well as good health, and by His stripes you *ARE* healed. The Scripture doesn't say, you will be healed, or you were healed, it says you *ARE* healed. I encourage you to hold on to that with every ounce of your faith, and every fiber of your being. Let God see that you trust Him. I really believe God wants to heal us, but sometimes it's because of our own lack of faith in His ability to do so. You know He can do it, but you wonder if He will do it for you.

Please don't listen to the lies of the enemy. William Murphy said in one of his songs, *"The devil couldn't tell the truth if he wanted to."* He is the father of lies. He will make everything seem worse than it really is. The moment you allow fear in, that same moment you compromise your faith. Rise up and be encouraged! Get in God's word and see what He is saying. Cancer didn't just form in my body. There were other doors that were open that allowed this disease to dwell. I dealt with anxiety and fear for many years; I had poor eating habits, as well as other contributing factors.

I also struggled with forgiving myself for things from my past and letting go of hurtful experiences. It was very important for me to recognize and ask God to heal me completely, not just my body, but also my soul and emotions. I had to cast out the spirit of fear, and accept God's love for me. Make sure your emotions are good. Wounded and damaged emotions can cause so much harm to our bodies. God is a God of wholeness and completeness. If you are holding a grudge against someone, let it go. Beverly M. Breaky wrote in her book, Choose Life, *"Forgiveness is a state of being, not a deed."* Forgiveness should be a natural part of what we do on a daily basis. The things stored up in your heart could be the very things that are making you sick.

Current day physicians rarely observe their patients for mental, spiritual, or emotional pain. If there is no medication to prescribe or surgery to perform, Western Medicine is at a loss. Sometimes the emotional and mental pain is worse than physical sickness. That's why I needed God to heal me completely. I pay more attention to how I'm feeling now. I express myself more, and I have asked God to remove the pain of my past. My personal goals now is to remain physically fit, eat right, stay connected to God, and to love and see myself the way God does. I am very grateful that God has chosen me as a vessel to work through.

Stand and Trust Him

"And they were overcome by the blood of the lamb and the word of their testimony" (Revelations 12:11). Because of this scripture, I will tell this story everywhere I go. I met a woman a couple of years

ago who told me to never let anyone silence me. She said to always share your story even if people get tired of hearing it. Someone will be encouraged and delivered by what you went through.

I have peace that I am covered in His blood. I strongly advise you to keep yourself covered. His blood is your protection. Outside of His blood, you're subject to anything. In the Old Testament, when blood was placed over the door, the death angel would pass over it. This journey has been long, but not as long as some. God spared me for such a time as this, and allowed the death angel to pass over me. When the enemy tried to take me out, God said no! My heart goes out to all the families that have lost loved ones to this disease.

Just know God has someone interceding on your behalf. I'm praying like countless others for God's continual comfort, and healing for you and your family. If you have been diagnosed, please remember God has the last say. I urge you to pursue God, because in Him you will find yourself, as well as your healing. Everything isn't of the enemy. God allows certain things to come our way to see how we hold up in the midst. His purpose for our life is greater than we can see. Faith is the key to anything you need from God. God can't lie and His Word is proven.

I read a passage of devotion by Sara Young that said, "*When you depend on God continually, your whole perspective changes. You see miracles happening all around, while others see only natural occurrences and coincidences. You begin each new day with joyful expectation, watching to see what He will do. You consciously live, move and have your being in Him, desiring that He lives in you, and you living in Him."*

It is through knowing God intimately that we become like Him. This requires spending time alone with Him. Let go, relax, be still, and allow Jesus to take the wheel. Our direction and guidance comes from Him only. The more time we spend in prayer, the less we need to seek answers from others. The only way to keep our lives in balance is to fix our eyes on Christ, and when this happen all fears and doubts are erased.

If and when you encounter a problem you feel you have no immediate solution to, one of two things will happen: either it will take you up in prayer, or down in despair. We always have a choice about how we respond to the difficulty in our lives. Our attitude is one of the main things that we can control. Be careful that you're not having a pity party while you're going through. Your attitude can either encourage others or discourage others. There were times I wanted to complain and ask, *"why me?"* But I knew too many people were watching, and more importantly, my faith encouraged so many others.

John Maxwell says there are two great events that happen in a person's life, *"One is when you are born and the other is when you find out why."* I realized the thing in life that infuriates you the most, is probably the area in which God is going to use you. We all must endure and stand strong as warriors, always remembering the battle is not ours but the Lord's.

I prayed that if it wasn't His will I endure certain things, that He would not allow it. I did by faith stand on the Word and declare it.

150

Sure, I did my part by eating right and exercising, but ultimately it was my faith in God's ability to heal me. If God said it in His word then I believe it, and so should you. It's that simple. You can't please God by being fearful and doubtful. It just won't happen. You will have to pull yourself together and decide whose report you are going to believe.

The battle is won first in your mind. As you read, I had a series of ups and downs in my faith. I bounced from faith to fear, but I knew that God was able. There will be moments of fear that you may have also, but don't stay there. Get yourself back on track and keep believing God.

I had to journey along and not get caught up in where I was going or when I was coming out. That was up to God. *"Knowing this, that the trying of your faith, worketh patience"* (James 1:3). I had come to realize it wasn't about how long it took me to come out, but it was about what was taking place on the inside of me. God was more concerned with my inner transformation than how I looked from the outside or how fast I got there. I heard a pastor say, *"You can't rush God,"* and that is so true. Everything has a fullness of time. When Jesus was born, it was indeed the fullness of time. God's plan was perfect and on point, just as His plan for you and me.

Don't miss out on your blessings because of weariness, or your lack of faith. Tremaine Hawkins has a song that says, *"I Never Lost my Praise."* In the midst of all of life's heartaches, always find a reason to praise God. Maybe you've experienced the death of a loved one. Instead of being mad at God, thank Him for the time you shared with that person. I met a woman in the store who wasn't able to forgive herself because she talked her mother into taking chemo. Her mother died during the treatments because her body wasn't strong enough to fight. This woman was living with guilt, blaming herself for her mother's death. God used me to speak to her about forgiveness. Once she was able to forgive herself, she was able to tell God, *"thank you,"* and focus on the good times she and her mother shared.

My Last Piece of Information

Here is a bit of information I want you to know and understand concerning your food. Often times the food manufacturers and the FDA won't tell you the truth about what's in your food. They know that if you really knew the ingredients in food products, you likely wouldn't purchase them.

Here's a couple of ingredients to watch out for when you're grocery shopping. If you come across these ingredients, it's very important that you refrain from buying it. This could be detrimental to you and your family's health.

- Sodium Nitrates-This is a dangerous ingredient with no warnings on the label of the packaged food. This ingredient can increase the risk of cancer by 67 percent. It's a preservative found in processed meats. Sodium nitrates gives food color, adds extra flavor, preserves the meat so it won't spoil as quickly, and controls bacterial growth.

- Hydrogenated oil or vegetable oil- can cause heart disease, nutritional decencies, diabetes, cancer, as well as other health problems. It is found in sweets such as cookies, crackers, manufactured foods, and margarine. It is used to keep shelf life for a longer period of time.
- Aspartame- This ingredient causes nerve damage and can be found in diet sodas, canned foods, breakfast sausage, salad dressings, chewing gum, and Crystal Light. This ingredient causes muscle spasms, depression, migraines, dizziness, difficulty breathing, and so many other dangerous side effects.
- High fructose corn syrup and sugar- Affects the immune system, causes depression, obesity, anxiety, diabetes, high blood pressure, and so many other health risks.
- White flour, artificial colors, and sweeteners should be avoided as well.

Here are a couple of spices that defend against cancer. When you're cooking, replace some of the other spices with these:

- Cinnamon- lowers cholesterol
- Turmeric- this is a strong prevention against colon, breast, lung, stomach, skin, and prostate cancer
- Oregano- has a lot of antioxidants that slows down the progression of cancer

- Garlic- assists in breast cancer and kills leukemia cells
- Ginger- helps against precancerous cells and prevents cancer causing compounds from forming in the body
- Rosemary- Reduces breast cancer by 76 percent

Some vegetables that are very healthy and high on the list to defend the body against cancer are:

- Broccoli, cauliflower, asparagus, and cabbage are especially potent against fighting cancer
- Fiber, beans, and red wine have also been known to fight cancer
- There are major benefits in consuming green tea, blueberries and recent studies have shown that dark chocolate is also beneficial
- A plant based diet is beneficial to staying healthy and defending your body against disease.

There are many natural herbs and supplements you can purchase from a whole food store that will be very beneficial to you. It could be there's some disease in your family that is genetic and you believe the curse has to be broken. Go ahead, get the heads up and start taking preventative measures now. The cancer in my case was reversible, but maybe in your case it could be prevented all together. Either way, knowledge and application is power. Get on the Internet. You will see a whole world of natural herbs and teas that are used to cure cancer and so many other diseases.

For anyone with cancer, Essiac Tea, also known as Flo Essence, is extremely beneficial in fighting cancer. I previously explained how this powerful cancer fighting tea came about. I recommend this tea to anyone who has cancer. It can be purchased from your local Whole Food Store, or any health food store. IP6, Vitamin B17, and Zeolite Enhanced with DHQ are also very good for cancer.

Find scriptures on healing, learn them, live them, believe them, and begin to profess them over your life. Your mouth is a weapon against the enemy. Open up your mouth, declare and decree life abundantly, good health, and break the spirit of sickness that could be hovering over you or your loved one. If you're not familiar with confessions, it's a good idea to learn more about them. I heard a pastor preach, *"Many Christians have stopped using profanity but they are still cursing."* It's something worth thinking about. Are you speaking blessings over your life, or curses?

We should be experiencing heaven right here on earth. I went through my time of suffering, and now I'm rejoicing. I believe God found me to be faithful. Will He find you faithful as you are faced with life's difficulties? Are you complaining and turning to everyone for help except God? Please check yourself and make sure your attitude is one of gratitude that will glorify the Father.

Whatever hurt your trials may bring, try to focus beyond the trial, to the blessings that follow. It's a blessing to be able to share your story, whatever it may be, and encourage the hearts of others. Our hurts and pain draws us closer to God, which should be our entire goal. Move forward and don't question, even as doubts may

155

enter your mind. Choose to trust God, and others will notice the light of Christ shining through you. Have you ever noticed during your greatest time of trials, someone will look at you and tell you that you're glowing? I've noticed that about people that I knew who were having hard times. Others have also told me that about myself as I was going through trials.

Most importantly stand in faith, believing that God is able. *"Without faith it's impossible to please God, for he who comes to Him must believe that He is, and that He is a rewarder of them that diligently Seek Him"* (Hebrew 11:6). His healing is available to you. Seek Him, cry out to Him, pursue your healing at all costs and begin to thank Him for a victorious outcome.

It is my prayer that you have come to know Christ as your personal Savior, and have surrendered your heart to Him and allowed Him to heal your mind, body and soul. I love you, and may the grace of God be with you!

"What do you conspire against the Lord? He will make an utter end of it. Affliction will not rise up a second time" (Nahum 1:9).

Cancer Shall Never Return in Jesus Name!

Keep looking out for the release of my next book:

From Survivor to OVERCOMER

The world calls you a survivor if you pull through life's adversities, however there's no victory in just pulling through. You must OVERCOME!

From Survivor to Overcomer is about adopting a victorious state of mind as you understand that you are God's highest form of creation. He has given each of us the extraordinary ability and the power to recreate our very existence by what we think and speak. It's about the mind of a champion and standing up in the midst of hard times with unshakable faith in God. This book will also teach you about faith, patience and hope and most of all to understand God's purpose for a victorious life for each of His children.

Author Contact Information

Reschelle Means- website www.intrudercalledcancer.net

Email- reschellem@yahoo.com

Facebook- Reschelle Means

Blog- reschellem.tumblr.com

For Other Services

Sharonda Brewer for graphic design-
sharondadbrewer@gmail.com

Ronald Goode for photos- ronaldegoode@gmail.com

KingdomatikVizionz@gmail.com

Disclaimer

I Reschelle Means am not a doctor, any information in this book is based on my faith in God, my opinion, extensive research and my own personal experience of healing myself using the herbs and the information that I share in this book. The data is meant for informational purposes only and not intended to serve as medical advice, substitute for a doctor's appointment, or to be used for diagnosing or treating a disease. If you or a love one is sick, please seek your health care provider.

All scripture is taken from the New King James Bible

Made in the USA
Charleston, SC
24 November 2015